Streetwise Safety for Women

by
Michael DePasquale Jr.

Charles E. Tuttle Co., Inc.
Boston • Rutland, Vermont • Tokyo

Published by Charles E. Tuttle Company, Inc. of Rutland, Vermont, and Tokyo, Japan with editorial offices at 153 Milk Street, Boston, Massachusetts 02109

Library of Congress Cataloging-in Publication Data
DePasquale, Michael.
      Streetwise safety for women / by Michael DePasquale, Jr.
          p.   cm. -- (Streetwise safety)
      ISBN 0-8048-3014-2
      1. Self-defense for women.   I. Title. II. Series.
GV1111.5.D46 1994   94-6863
613.6′6--dc20   CIP

First Edition

1 3 5 7 9 10 8 6 4 2

Printed in the United States of America

Disclaimer

Please note that the publisher of this instructional book is not responsible in any manner whatsoever for any injury that may result from practicing the techniques and/or following the instructions given within. Since the physical activities described herein may be too strenuous in nature for some readers to engage in safely, *it is essential that a physician be consulted prior to training.*

This book is dedicated to the woman in my life, my mother, Josephine DePasquale, who has been a true inspiration in my life and was always there when I needed encouragement and still is. I would also like to acknowledge the support of the rest of my family including my grandmother, Giovanna DeLuise, my Aunt Rose and Aunt Margie. And of course, to all the WOMEN I have done programs for throughout the country and abroad. It's about time WOMEN finally take a stand and realize the importance of Streetwise safety around the world.

SPECIAL ACKNOWLEDGEMENTS

Special thanks is due to my father, Michael DePasquale, Sr. for his knowledge and help in the crime prevention and self-defense areas. I would also like to thank my staff who helped make this book possible, Mark Piano, Gail Miller, Dotty Pillisher, Monica Schulman and Eileen Muenchen. I would also like to thank Terri Lebowitz and Chris Shoolis for their photography, Mark Piano and Ed Salter for art direction and illustration.

Models appearing in this book include: David James, Terri Lebowitz, Monica Schulman, Nancy Allen, Josephine DePasquale, Chris Schoolis, Jorge Espinosa, Lisa Donato, Tom Linaris, John Turbridy, Stan Fixler and Frank Buonocore.

A special thanks to "Crime Prevention Consultants and Security Experts," Bill D'Urso, Robert Suggs, Richard Dillon, Rick Fike, Michael DePasquale, Sr. and Tom Patire for their assistance.

GENERAL ACKNOWLEDGMENTS

It would be very difficult for us to identify many of the sources for the "Crime Prevention and Self Defense" information used to create this book, but we would like to thank those departments, organizations and reference books that made this publication an actuality:

The New York City Police Department
United States Department of Justice
The Federal Bureau of Investigation
National Criminal of Justice Information and
Statistic Service International Protection Inc.
Interdome Group Inc.
State of the Art Security
The Truth About Self Protection
How to Protect Yourself From Crime
How to Keep From Being Robbed Raped & Ripped Off
Total Self-Protection

Here at last is the book we have all been waiting for! It is clear, concise and complete, and has been written in such manner as to be a must for everyone seeking to protect herself, her home or family. This volume is born of years of personal experience in the security field. My son Michael DePasquale is highly trained and skillful in the area of unarmed combat. His method of teaching is vibrant and yet highly technical. He has developed a system of instruction that results in a layman blocking and striking an attacker with such speed and balance that one could easily miss the movements employed. He has instructed people from numerous organizations, such as peace officers from municipal, county, state and federal offices. Additionally, he has been called upon to instruct members of the army's first division special forces and other highly mobile and combat-ready military units. He has become a legend as an instructor, and everyone who has had the good fortune to receive his personal attention leaves the training hall in much the same manner as an ancient Roman gladiator must have left the arena after dispatching his opponents. Michael possesses that unique ability not only to instruct a student in the art of combat, but also to plant a seed of enthusiasm that immediately bursts forth and mentally prepares the defender for decisive action.

The techniques he demonstrates are straight to the point, highly effective and directed at the attacker's weakest point. Many self defense techniques are discussed in chapters: 7, 8 and 9. This touchy and very important section of the book clearly defines situations that have blossomed into problems that are becoming more common. The information furnished in chapter 6 ranges from child abuse to domestic violence. This chapter alone is worth the price of this volume. The subject of abuse is one that should be understood by everyone. When faced with any form of abuse, an individual should understand his or her position. Chapter 6 should be read carefully. The information on rape as covered in chapter 7 is clearly presented in a simple form that is easily understood. The advice: "don't be a victim," grows more and more important each day. It is a subject that grows with the population. In chapter 8, I find a wealth of information, and it is truly a text for self- training. Adoption of these suggestions will make the reader less vulnerable to attack. Once the reader understands the problems listed, she will be in a better position to defend herself and her family. To this end, the writer has most effectively defined the situations as necessary. Again, in chapter 8, the subject of using a weapon, such as a knife or club, is most clearly explained and should be readily understood by any reader.

Chapter 9 clearly explains basic techniques, strikes to vulnerable areas, use of personal items as weapons of self defense, attack and counter attack. All begin to make more and more sense as one reads on. I liked the subjects: "how to prevent injuries," and "a word about nutrition."

I purposely left chapters 1, Statistics, Chapter 2, Home Security, and chapter 3, Potential danger in the workplace for last. Chapter 1 gives a wealth of information that shows the reader just how dangerous this society has become.

Everyday danger rises as time marches on. The statistics clearly show the need for self-preservation through a knowledge of the crime situation and the many steps we can take for self and family protection. Reading this book highlights the necessity of : reporting crime and watching out for suspicious activity which is quite often the beginning of an attack. Strangers at your door may well develop into intruders in your home, at which time your telephone becomes an important source of security.

With very few words, the writer has skillfully included information on lighting your home. Too many people are extremely lax in this regard, and during hours of darkness they become the subject of attack. The information on the subject of a neighborhood watch should be well received by any reader. This subject is timely, and quite effective in many parts of the country where such organizations are in operation, often linking themselves with other groups. In chapter 3, we find subjects such as "Potential Danger In The Workplace." There is a very vulnerable time period between the time one is at work and the time he or she is at home. Leaving the work place building and entering the parking lot and then an auto places the individual at a distinct disadvantage if he is ignorant of the potential danger, or of what action to take if attacked. A treasure of information on the subjects of "Taxicabs," "Subways & Trains" and "Traveling By Air" prepares the reader for almost any eventuality. I must admit, this is one of the finest books on the subject of security that I have ever had the pleasure of reading.

BY MICHAEL DEPASQUALE SR.
Dai Shihan Yoshitsune Ju Jitsu
United States Army Criminal Investigation Division
Polygraphist
Retired Railroad Police
State Licensed Private Detective
Founder International Protection Systems Inc.
Lecturer, Terrorism And Explosives
US Government Security Agents

CONTENTS

The following statistics were obtained from the U.S. Department of Justice, "Crime in the United States 1992".

Among female murder victims, 29% were slain by their husbands or boyfriends, while 4% of male victims were killed by their wives or girlfriends. Firearms were the weapons used in approximately 7 out of every 10 murders. 12% of murder victims in general were related to their assailant, with 35% of victims were acquainted to them.

Rapes by force constitued the greatest percentages of rape, at 86%. The remainder were attempts or assaults to commit forcible rape.

Aggravated assault is an unlawful attack by one person upon another for the purpose of inflicting severe or aggravated bodily injury. There were 442 reported victims of aggravated assault for every 100,000 people nationwide. 31% of them were committed with blunt objects, 26% used personal weapons such as hands, fists, and feet, 25% involved firearms, with knives bringing up the remainder.

Property crimes such as burglary, larceny, theft, motor vehicle theft, and arson produced a total monetary loss of 15.2 billion dollars for the country as a whole. The average loss per offense was approximately $1,217. Two out of every three burglaries were residential in nature. 69% of these involved forcible entry. The average loss for a residential offense was $1,215. The average loss for purse-snatching was $292, and for pick-pockets was $430.

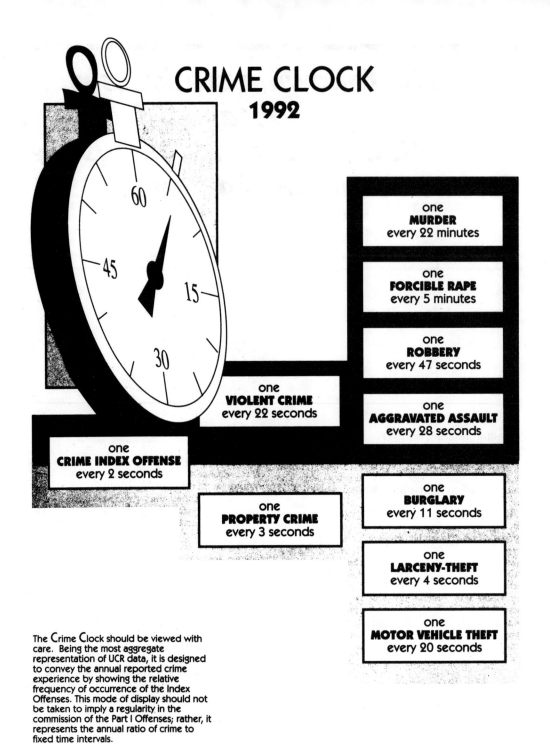

CRIME CLOCK
1992

one
MURDER
every 22 minutes

one
FORCIBLE RAPE
every 5 minutes

one
ROBBERY
every 47 seconds

one
VIOLENT CRIME
every 22 seconds

one
AGGRAVATED ASSAULT
every 28 seconds

one
CRIME INDEX OFFENSE
every 2 seconds

one
BURGLARY
every 11 seconds

one
PROPERTY CRIME
every 3 seconds

one
LARCENY-THEFT
every 4 seconds

one
MOTOR VEHICLE THEFT
every 20 seconds

The Crime Clock should be viewed with care. Being the most aggregate representation of UCR data, it is designed to convey the annual reported crime experience by showing the relative frequency of occurrence of the Index Offenses. This mode of display should not be taken to imply a regularity in the commission of the Part I Offenses; rather, it represents the annual ratio of crime to fixed time intervals.

CALENDAR YEAR 1992
STATISTICAL NOTES

1. Generally, the tables ranking the 10 or 25 largest cities by crime rate per 100,000 population list the 10 or 25 cities in the U.S. by populations. However, if the FBI crime statistics are unavailable for any of the 10 or 25 largest cities, that city will be replaced by the next largest city—by population—for which crime statistics are available. It should also be noted that the 10 or 25 largest cities list will change from year to year as the population of specific cities increases or decreases, thus moving that city into or out of the 10 or 25 largest cities group.

2. Population of the cities reflects data from the FBI annual publication Crime in the United States (1991).

3. Phoenix, the 9th largest city, was not included in the rankings for this analysis; this city was not listed in the FBI's Calendar Year 1992 Uniform Crime Report.

4. Chicago, the 3rd largest city in population, was not ranked for the calendar-year of 1992. Total Index Crime for Chicago was not listed in the FBI's annual release, because Forcible Rape figures furnished by the State level Uniform Crime Reporting (UCR) Program administered by the Illinois Department of State Police were not in accordance with the national UCR guidelines. If Chicago had been ranked in its reported crime categories, the result would have been as follows:

NYC WITH CHICAGO ADDED			NYC WITHOUT CHICAGO ADDED
MURDER	6	11	10
ROBBERY	2	4	3
AGGR. ASSAULT	1	10	9
BURGLARY	13	22	22
LARCENY THEFT	12	22	22
M.V. THEFT	13	11	11

5. Indianapolis and Denver, the 26th and 27th largest cities respectively, replaced Chicago (the 3rd) and Phoenix (the 9th) largest cities for this analysis.

CRIME INDEX TRENDS
CALENDAR YEAR 1992

1. Nationwide percentage changes in crime compared to New York City for the same period of time:

NATIONWIDE	CRIME	NEW YORK CITY
-6	MURDER & NON-NEGLIGENT MANSLAUGHTER	-7.4
+2	FORCIBLE RAPE	-2.7
-3	ROBBERY	-7.4
+2	AGGRAVATED ASSAULT	-4.9
0	VIOLENT CRIME VS PERSONS	-6.3
-6	BURGLARY	-7.6
-4	LARCENY THEFT	-7.9
-4	MOTOR VEHICLE THEFT	-9.3
-4	CRIMES VS PROPERTY	-8.2
-4	TOTAL CRIME INDEX	-7.8

2. Ranking by *percentage increase/decrease*, Total Crime Index, for the TEN largest cities. (See Statistical Notes)

RANK CAL. YEAR 1992	CITY	%CHANGE CAL. YEAR 1992	RANK CAL. YEAR 1991	%CHANGE CAL. YEAR 1991
1	BALTIMORE	+5.9	2	+9.1
2	LOS ANGELES	-2.2	3	+7.7
3	SAN DIEGO	-4.7	10	-4.7
4	SAN JOSE	-7.1	1	+12.5
5	SAN ANTONIO	-7.1	5	+0.6
6	DETROIT	-7.7	4	+1.4
7	NEW YORK	-7.8	9	-4.4
8	PHILADELPHIA	-10.8	8	-4.3
9	DALLAS	-16.0	6	-0.9
10	HOUSTON	-17.8	7	-2.5

3. New York City ranking per 100,000 population for calendar year 1992 & 1991.

In crime rate per 100,000 population for the seven major crimes (Crime Index Trends), New York City ranks as follows among the TWENTY-FIVE largest cities. Note: City with highest rate of crime per 100,000 population ranks 1st; City with lowest rate of crime ranks 25th.

CALENDAR YEAR	1992	1991
MURDER AND NON-NEGLIGENT MANSLAUGHTER	10TH	9th
FORCIBLE RAPE	24TH	24TH
ROBBERY	3RD	2ND
AGGRAVATED ASSAULT	9TH	10TH
BURGLARY	22ND	21ST
LARCENY-THEFT	22ND	21ST
MOTOR VEHICLE THEFT	11TH	10TH
TOTAL CRIME INDEX	8TH	16TH

RANKING PER 100,000 POPULATION, TOTAL CRIME INDEX—TEN LARGEST CITIES YEAR END 1992

RANK	CITY	RATE
1	DALLAS	12649.3
2	BALTIMORE	12045.9
3	SAN ANTONIO	11416.7
4	DETROIT	11315.0
5	LOS ANGELES	9513.8
6	HOUSTON	8901.9
7	NEW YORK	8519.5
8	SAN DIEGO	8137.9
9	PHILADELPHIA	6097.5
10	SAN JOSE	4984.3

RANKING PER 100,000 POPULATION, TOTAL CRIME INDEX TWENTY-FIVE LARGEST CITIES YEAR END 1992

RANK	CITY	RATE
1	DALLAS	12649.3
2	SEATTLE	12283.6
3	BALTIMORE	12045.9
4	SAN ANTONIO	11416.7
5	DETROIT	11315.0
6	WASHINGTON D.C.	11249.3
7	JACKSONVILLE	10624.7
8	SAN FRANCISCO	10358.2
9	NEW ORLEANS	10072.3
10	MEMPHIS	9989.8
11	BOSTON	9852.3
12	NASHVILLE	9828.6
13	LOS ANGELES	9513.8
14	EL PASO	9204.1
15	COLUMBUS	9117.9
16	HOUSTON	8901.9
17	MILWAUKEE	8761.3
18	NEW YORK	8519.5
19	DENVER	8379.3
20	CLEVELAND	8342.1
21	SAN DIEGO	8137.9
22	LAS VEGAS	7599.1
23	INDIANAPOLIS	7327.1
24	PHILADELPHIA	6097.5
25	SAN JOSE	4984.3

CRIME INDEX TRENDS AS REPORTED TO THE F.B.I. —TEN LARGEST CITIES YEAR END 1992 VS 1991—MURDER & NON-NEGL. MANSLAUGHTER

CITY	1992	1991	PERCENT
NEW YORK	1995	2154	-7.4
LOS ANGELES	1095	1027	6.6
HOUSTON	465	608	-23.5
PHILADELPHIA	425	440	-3.4
SAN DIEGO	146	167	-12.6
DETROIT	600	615	-2.4
DALLAS	386	500	-22.8
SAN ANTONIO	218	208	4.8
SAN JOSE	43	53	-18.9
BALTIMORE	336	304	10.5

FORCIBLE RAPE

CITY	1992	1991	PERCENT
NEW YORK	2815	2892	-2.7
LOS ANGELES	1872	1966	-4.8
HOUSTON	1169	1213	-3.6
PHILADELPHIA	781	904	-13.6
SAN DIEGO	485	472	2.8
DETROIT	1225	1427	-14.2
DALLAS	1096	1208	-9.3
SAN ANTONIO	616	698	-11.7
SAN JOSE	448	445	0.7
BALTIMORE	749	701	6.8

ROBBERY

CITY	1992	1991	PERCENT
NEW YORK	91239	98512	-7.4
LOS ANGELES	39508	39778	-0.7
HOUSTON	11130	13883	-19.8
PHILADELPHIA	11681	13921	-16.1
SAN DIEGO	5321	5331	-0.2
DETROIT	12194	13569	-10.1
DALLAS	9532	11254	-15.3
SAN ANTONIO	3485	3778	-7.8
SAN JOSE	1231	1328	-7.3
BALTIMORE	12263	10770	13.9

AGGRAVATED ASSAULT

CITY	1992	1991	PERCENT
NEW YORK	63529	66832	-4.9
LOS ANGELES	46445	47104	-1.4
HOUSTON	12073	10947	10.3
PHILADELPHIA	6180	7216	-14.4
SAN DIEGO	8840	7860	12.5
DETROIT	12433	12651	-1.7
DALLAS	10667	13449	-20.7
SAN ANTONIO	2811	2889	-2.7
SAN JOSE	3705	3432	8.0
BALTIMORE	8452	7257	16.5

BURGLARY

CITY	1992	1991	PERCENT
NEW YORK	103476	112015	-7.6
LOS ANGELES	57771	57460	0.5
HOUSTON	30207	39726	-24.0
PHILADELPHIA	16199	21460	-24.5
SAN DIEGO	16437	17088	-3.8
DETROIT	22048	26059	-15.4
DALLAS	24806	31513	-21.3
SAN ANTONIO	21967	24941	-11.9
SAN JOSE	6776	7403	-8.5
BALTIMORE	16298	16230	0.4

LARCENY THEFT

CITY	1992	1991	PERCENT
NEW YORK	236169	256473	-7.9

MOTOR VEHICLE THEFT

CITY	1992	1991	PERCENT
NEW YORK	12659	139977	-9.3
LOS ANGELES	67981	68655	-1.0
HOUSTON	30938	40162	-23.0
PHILADELPHIA	22416	24318	-7.8
SAN DIEGO	20231	21218	-4.7
DETROIT	27344	28740	-4.9
DALLAS	20515	25085	-18.2
SAN ANTONIO	14722	14413	2.1
SAN JOSE	3793	4512	-15.9
BALTIMORE	11300	10593	6.7

TOTAL CRIME INDEX

CITY	1992	1991	PERCENT
NEW YORK	626182	678855	-7.8
LOS ANGELES	338532	346224	-2.2
HOUSTON	148284	180308	-17.8
PHILADELPHIA	97359	109139	-10.8
SAN DIEGO	92258	96781	-4.7
DETROIT	117251	127080	-7.7
DALLAS	130081	154929	-16.0
SAN ANTONIO	109133	117486	-7.1
SAN JOSE	39802	42836	-7.1
BALTIMORE	90115	85068	5.9

RANKING BY % INCREASE OR DECREASE IN CRIME TEN LARGEST CITIES YEAR END 1992 1992 VS 1991

RANK	CITY	MURDER & NON-NEG. MANSLAUGHTER
1	BALTIMORE	10.5
2	LOS ANGELES	6.6
3	SAN ANTONIO	4.9
4	DETROIT	-2.4
5	PHILADELPHIA	-3.4
6	NEW YORK	-7.4
7	SAN DIEGO	-12.6
8	SAN JOSE	-18.9
9	DALLAS	-22.8
10	HOUSTON	-23.5

RANK	CITY	FORCIBLE RAPE
1	BALTIMORE	6.8
2	SAN DIEGO	2.8
3	SAN JOSE	0.7
4	NEW YORK	-2.7
5	HOUSTON	-3.6
6	LOS ANGELES	-4.8
7	DALLAS	-9.3

	SAN ANTONIO	-11.7
8		
9	PHILADELPHIA	-13.6
10	DETROIT	-14.2

RANK	CITY	ROBBERY
3	SAN DIEGO	-4.7
4	SAN JOSE	-7.1
5	SAN ANTONIO	-7.1
6	DETROIT	-7.7
7	NEW YORK	-7.8
8	PHILADELPHIA	-10.8
9	DALLAS	-16.0
10	HOUSTON	-17.8

RANKING OF THE TEN LARGEST CITIES BY RATE PER 100,000 —POPULATION FOR THE YEAR END 1992—MURDER & NON-NEG. MANSLAUGHTER

RANK	CITY	RATE
1	DETROIT	57.9
2	BALTIMORE	44.9
3	DALLAS	37.5
4	LOS ANGELES	30.8
5	HOUSTON	27.9
6	NEW YORK	27.1
7	PHILADELPHIA	26.6
8	SAN ANTONIO	22.8
9	SAN DIEGO	12.9
10	SAN JOSE	5.4

FORCIBLE RAPE

RANK	CITY	RATE
1	DETROIT	118.2
2	DALLAS	106.6
3	BALTIMORE	100.1
4	HOUSTON	70.2
5	SAN ANTONIO	64.4
6	SAN JOSE	56.1
7	LOS ANGELES	52.6
8	PHILADELPHIA	48.9
9	SAN DIEGO	42.8
10	NEW YORK	38.3

ROBBERY

RANK	CITY	RATE
1	BALTIMORE	1639.2
2	NEW YORK	1241.3
3	DETROIT	1176.7
4	LOS ANGELES	1110.3
5	DALLAS	926.9
6	PHILADELPHIA	731.6
7	HOUSTON	668.2
8	SAN DIEGO	469.4
9	SAN ANTONIO	364.6
10	SAN JOSE	154.2

AGGRAVATED ASSAULT

RANK	CITY	RATE

1	LOS ANGELES	1305.3
2	DETROIT	1199.8
3	BALTIMORE	1129.9
4	DALLAS	1037.3
5	NEW YORK	864.3
6	SAN DIEGO	779.8
7	HOUSTON	724.8
8	SAN JOSE	464.0
9	PHILADELPHIA	294.1

BURGLARY

RANK	CITY	RATE
1	DALLAS	2414.2
2	SAN ANTONIO	2298.0
3	BALTIMORE	2178.5
4	DETROIT	2127.7
5	HOUSTON	1813.4
6	LOS ANGELES	1623.5
7	SAN DIEGO	1449.9
8	NEW YORK	1407.8
9	PHILADELPHIA	1014.5
10	SAN JOSE	848.5

LARCENY THEFT

RANK	CITY	RATE
1	SAN ANTONIO	6832.7
2	DALLAS	6133.9
3	BALTIMORE	5442.7
4	DETROIT	3995.9
5	HOUSTON	3740.2
6	SAN DIEGO	3598.7
7	LOS ANGELES	3480.9
8	NEW YORK	3213.2
9	SAN JOSE	2981.2
10	PHILADELPHIA	2484.9

MOTOR VEHICLE THEFT

RANK	CITY	RATE
1	DETROIT	2638.8
2	DALLAS	1994.9
3	LOS ANGELES	1910.5
4	HOUSTON	1857.3
5	SAN DIEGO	1784.5
6	NEW YORK	1727.3
7	SAN ANTONIO	1540.1
8	BALTIMORE	1510.5
9	PHILADELPHIA	1403.9
10	SAN JOSE	475.0

TOTAL CRIME INDEX

RANK	CITY	RATE
1	DALLAS	12649.3
2	BALTIMORE	12045.9
3	SAN ANTONIO	11416.7
4	DETROIT	11315.0
5	LOS ANGELES	9513.8
6	HOUSTON	8901.9
7	NEW YORK	8519.5
8	SAN DIEGO	8137.9
9	PHILADELPHIA	6097.5
10	SAN JOSE	4984.3

COMPARISON OF TEN LARGEST CITIES YEAR END 1992 —BY POPULATION AND CRIME INDEX AS REPORTED TO F.B.I.— NEW YORK CITY POPULATION AND CRIME INDEX AS A BASE

CITY	POPULATION	TOTAL CRIME INDEX
NEW YORK	7,350,023	626,182
LOS ANGELES	3,558,316	338,532
HOUSTON	1,665,756	148,284
PHILADELPHIA	1,596,699	97,359
SAN DIEGO	1,133,681	92,258
DETROIT	1,036,246	117,251
DALLAS	1,028,362	130,081
SAN ANTONIO	955,905	109,133
SAN JOSE	798,542	39,802
BALTIMORE	748,099	90,115

CITY	% POPULATION TO NYC	% OF CRIME TO NYC
NEW YORK	100.0%	100.0%
LOS ANGELES	48.4%	54.1%
HOUSTON	22.7%	23.7%
PHILADELPHIA	21.7%	15.5%
SAN DIEGO	15.4%	14.7%
DETROIT	14.1%	18.7%
DALLAS	14.0%	20.8%
SAN ANTONIO	13.0%	17.4%
SAN JOSE	10.9%	6.4%
BALTIMORE	10.2%	14.4%

Potential Danger In Your Home Environment

HOME SECURITY

Many crimes committed in the home or apartment could be avoided with proper precautions. A systematic check of all potentially dangerous, vulnerable areas in your home environment is needed on a daily basis.

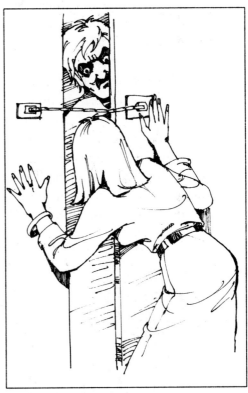

Naturally, it is impossible to predict where and when a crime will occur. Most of us would like to think crime won't happen to us. But it is still up to each of us to realize there is much we can do to create a safer, controlled home environment. Ultimately the responsibility lies with you and me.

Coming home to find your home or apartment has been robbed is bad enough. It is far worse, however, to interrupt a criminal in the midst of robbing your home, or to be home when the criminal attempts to enter.

First I will identify and discuss vulnerable areas of the home in order to help you prevent crime. Later, I will explore defensive tactics you can successfully apply, should they be required.

LOCKS

It is practically impossible to prevent a criminal from entering your house or apartment through an outside door if the criminal has the determination, skills and the time to do so. Remember, a criminal wants to spend the least amount of time and effort in the illegal act as possible. Making it difficult for him to enter is often enough to deter him and send him on his way, to an easier target. Sometimes all you need is the proper type of door and window locks.

DOORS

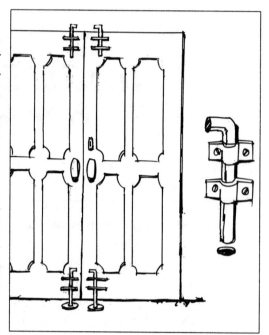

Your doors should be locked at all times. Each door to your home should have a peep-hole or wide angle viewer. The ideal arrangement would be a solid wooden door or a hollow metal door snugly fit in its frame, secured with dead-bolt locks and double-cylinder locks. A dead-bolt lock is superior to most other locks because it cannot be forced open with a knife, spatula, or similar tool. If the dead bolt is sufficiently long, 1 1/2 inches or more, the door becomes nearly impossible to jimmy open. There are a number of excellent dead bolt locks presently available on the market and I recommend you install one on each outside door to supplement whatever locking devices you are presently using. A double-cylinder lock is especially useful for doors with glass or wooden panels. This lock requires a key from both the outside and inside, thus preventing an intruder from reaching through broken glass or a broken panel to unlock the door from the inside.

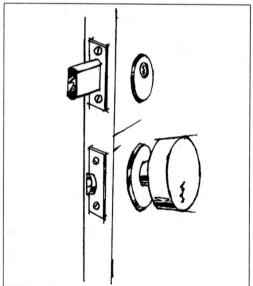

However, heed a word of caution about double-cylinder locks: In the event of fire or similar emergency, double-cylinder locks can delay occupants from exiting the house. Therefore, a key to the inside lock must be readily at hand, always.

WINDOWS

All windows of your home or apartment should have their own locking devices. Key locks work best. When possible, protect windows with metal grillwork or metal bars. Further, you can use break-resistant glass to increase the security of your windows. Examine the windows in your home or apartment to determine how effective their locks are. If there are any vulnerable win-

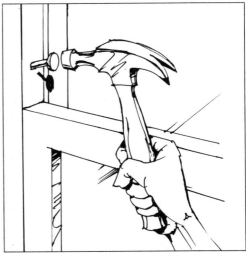

dows, specific locks may be needed to rectify the situation. Check with a security specialist or your local police department for helpful suggestions. An effective and simple way to secure your windows is to drill a slanted hole through the bottom window frame, or sash, halfway through the top frame (do not drill completely through the outside frame) and insert a metal pin or nail. This will prevent the window from being opened from the outside.

A window air conditioner represents a vulnerable spot. Be certain your window air conditioner is securely mounted and attached to its window frame. The same applies to sliding doors or windows, and outside

patio or vestibule doors and windows; be certain they snugly fit their frames. An enclosed patio or vestibule provides a secure work space for an intruder, and often the locks on patio windows or doors aren't as sound as those on the home itself.

Place as many obstacles as you can between an intruder and your home. Be certain details aren't overlooked. For example, sheds and garages are often secured with a padlock. But a padlock is only a deterrent because it can be pried or cut off quickly.

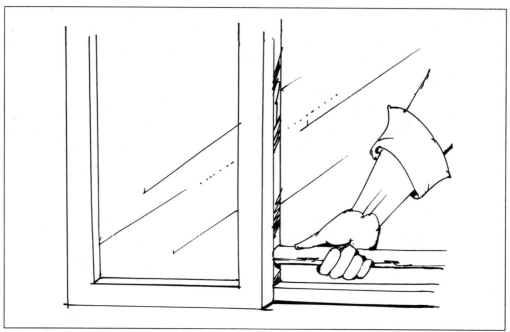

SLIDING GLASS DOORS

Sliding doors can be pried open easily so it's important to secure them. A steel rod or length of wood placed in the lower door track will prevent these doors from being opened. Also, a few screws drilled into the upper door track prevent the door from being lifted off and out of its tracks, which is another way an intruder might attempt to gain entry.

ALARMS

There are many home and business security systems available today. Determine the value of what you wish to protect; then you can decide what's right for you. If you do decide to get an alarm, I suggest you shop around before making your choice. After all, an alarm signals only when an intruder is entering or exiting your home. If your property is properly secured, the intruder may not be able to enter in the first place.

There are three basic alarm systems:

1. Local: Designed to alert persons inside a specific locale. This will generally frighten off intruders while alerting those present of possible danger.
2. Central or Remote: Designed to transmit signals to local police or security personnel. The police or security personnel will then investigate the alarm.

3: Proprietary: Designed to alarm a security force already in place within the location of the alarm. These systems are often used by warehouse or apartment complexes, providing security to property and residents.

REPORTING

Many crimes could be prevented if people would phone the police at the first sign of suspicious activity. Time is important, so report the crime or activity *immediately*.

Provide the police with all pertinent information: the address of the suspicious activity, the nature of it, and a complete description of any suspects or vehicles used. If reporting a crime, remember to provide police with your name, address and phone number.

SUSPICIOUS ACTIVITY

Suspicious activity can include a lot of behavior which is not considered normal by most standards. Some are obvious, some more subtle and less detectable, yet all should be considered and reported. Here are some examples of suspicious activity:

1. An unfamiliar vehicle repeatedly driving through your neighborhood, or one that stops and offers rides to children.
2. Anyone attempting to conceal him or herself behind objects.
3. An unfamiliar parked car with an occupant observing a home or residents.
4. Furniture being loaded into a van when you are in doubt about the home occupants being present.
5. A person peeking in windows.
6. A person running from a home or apartment building.
7. A person screaming.
8. Someone attempting to gain access to a home or car using force.

FAMILY SECURITY PROCEDURES

The key to family security lies in participation. All family members should help by discussing each other's lifestyles to point out potential vulnerabilities.

One family member may have insight into another's potential threats. By opening the conversation to all family members, including children, a greater variety of topics can be discussed, and an attitude of group participation is encouraged. Develop a family security checklist, and get everyone involved. At the end of this chapter you will find a suggested checklist for home security.

THE TELEPHONE

Believe it or not, the telephone represents a serious vulnerable spot in your home security. Although originally designed as an innocent instrument of communication, the telephone is often used as an instrument of crime. By using the telephone, a person can have access to vital information you wouldn't normally disclose. Anyone who is persuasive, friendly and tactful can get you to divulge private information.

Never reveal that your spouse is out of town, or gone for any length of time. Tell a caller your husband or father is expected back any moment, and offer to return the call. Never provide your name, number or address to strangers. If the caller persists, hang up. Under no circumstances should you ever provide personal information such as which bank you deal with, how much money is in your savings account, your account number, or any other financial information even if the caller identifies him or her self as a bank or credit official. Never answer telephone surveys. Request the caller to send you a written questionnaire if he or she wishes. Don't be tricked into revealing a credit card number to anyone claiming you have won a prize. This is a common way for a criminal to charge expenses to your account. If you won a contest, you must have entered it, and most contest winners are notified by mail.

As a precautionary measure, exchange telephone numbers with a neighbor you can trust, in case of an emergency. If you live alone, you could try a daily call-in routine. This way, if your neighbor doesn't hear from you, he or she will check on you to verify your safety. It is also a good idea to have emergency numbers taped to your phone, so you don't have to search for them in the event of a crisis.

Do not list your first name in the telephone directory. If you must have a listed number, your first initial along with your last name should be sufficient. Thus, anyone attempting to determine if you are a woman alone will not be able to do so. If you have children, do not allow them to answer the phone. Children are more easily tricked into revealing information, such as who is presently at home. Also, do not give out information to someone claiming your name was given to them as a reference. You can return their call once you verify their claim. Normally anyone using you as a reference is obliged to inform you in advance. Finally, hang up on all obscene or prank callers immediately, and report the call to the police and phone company. If such calls persist, do not engage in any type of conversation with the caller. Instead, inform authorities of the calls; they might wish to trace them.

INTRUDERS IN YOUR HOME

Coming home and encountering an intruder is very frightening. Regardless of whether the intruder is aware of your presence or not, this is

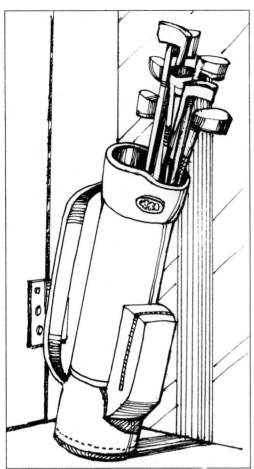

a most hazardous situation. No one really plans for such an occurrence; yet what would you do if it happened to you?

Naturally, your first impulse would be fright combined with anger, and a desire to protect yourself and your possessions. Suppress any desire to frighten the intruder away by yelling or other measures. Run to a neighbor's house, call the police, and await their arrival. You might consider alerting other neighbors while you wait for the police at your neighbor's house.

As scary as it is to come home and find an intruder there, the most frightening scenario, is being home alone, or in bed, while an intruder enters your house. If you are startled awake, and suspect an intruder is trying to force his way in, and visually confirm this, call the police and turn on every light you can in an attempt to frighten him away. Gather up any family members and exit via the opposite side of the house the intruder is entering.

If for any reason you cannot exit, hide someplace that, if possible, affords you a view of the intruder's entrance. Arm yourself with a baseball bat, poker, golf club, or gun if you have one. Once the intruder has entered, shout a warning that you have called the police, and inform him you are armed and will use your weapon if he continues. Normally things won't go this far because any intruder with common sense will retreat when the lights go on.

If you are in bed and an intruder enters, pretend you are asleep until you can escape, lock the door, or call the police. Hopefully the intruder will quietly go about his business and leave. If the intruder has intentions other than burglary, such as rape or assault, you will be faced with a very difficult decision: to resist or consent to his demands?

This is entirely your decision, based on your judgement of the situation. No one can recommend which choice you should make. If you resist, you must do so in a way which minimizes harm to you and maximizes your chance for escape. The first thing you can have in your favor is the element of surprise. To take advantage of this, you must have a weapon under your pillow or mattress such as a club, a firearm or knife. If the intruder is approaching you, make no sudden moves until he is within arms' reach.

Once the intruder is within your reach, attack him with all your might until your safety is secured. The intruder is threatening your life. Unless you are capable of violent action, he could disarm you and use your weapon against you. If you have no choice but to consent, it isn't because you chose to be assaulted, but that you had no other option. Often the safety and security of children nearby will be a deciding factor in such cases.

I recommend establishing a defensive plan involving each family member, household employees and babysitters against possible intruders. This will better enable you to prepare for any situation that may arise. Defensive tactics for such situations will be covered later on in this book.

STRANGERS AT THE DOOR

Don't admit anyone into your home or apartment unless they are familiar to you. A stranger's identity must be verified first. A peephole or viewer will help you by allowing you to see the stranger while he is still outside. You might also want to consider installing an intercom, especially if you live alone. This will allow you to speak with visitors without admitting them. If your home or apartment is equipped with a buzzer to admit callers, use it with discrimination. Never admit someone sight-unseen, especially if you live alone or are alone at the time. Assume the caller is falsifying his identity. Make sure at least one piece of ID has a picture of

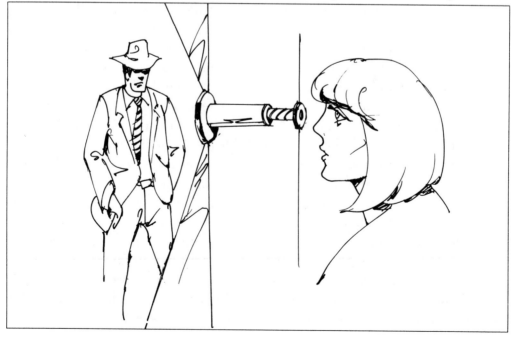

the caller. This also applies to police personnel. If a man calls, asking to read your meter, make him wait outside while you call his employer to verify the reading. If you have a door viewer and an intercom system, all of these precautions can be taken while the caller is still safely locked outside. Equal precautions should be taken regarding door-to-door salesmen, etc., and even professional persons with whom you have made an appointment. Take the time to call their offices to verify their identity.

Thieves and burglars will attempt to lure you from your home in many ways. Be aware of this. You could be lured from your home on the pretense of a lunch or business meeting, while your home is being robbed. Use your phone as a security measure. If you can verify a person's identity by his business listing in a public phone directory, chances are he is who he claims to be.

EMPLOYEES AND GUESTS

The term "home employees" covers a broad spectrum of persons, from the mailman to the domestic servant. All these individuals have access to your home on a regular basis and have knowledge of your activities. They acquire knowledge about your personal idiosyncrasies and habits that can put you at a disadvantage. Should one of these persons develop a grievance against you, he or she could have motivation and opportunity to rob or hurt you.

Take advantage of simple, common sense precautions to counter or prevent such a scenario. Check references and investigate. Bonded domestic employees may be more expensive, but the bond provides you a background check which somewhat protects you against dishonest acts.

Employment agencies also tend to supply more reputable employees, provided the employment agency itself isn't a "fly-by-night" company. Check with the Better Business Bureau for complaints against any agency you are considering. Look in the Yellow Pages to see if they were listed in the last year's book and have stood the test of time. If you're hiring an independent person, verify his or her references thoroughly. If a prospective employee cannot supply you with a complete list of personal and business references, do not hire that person. You cannot be too careful.

The same precautions apply to babysitters, painters, carpenters, repairmen and decorators. These persons represent the greater security hazard because they are often the employees of someone with whom you may have some sort of contractual agreement for a service. You cannot properly investigate such persons individually, and they may have access to your valuables while in your home. Lock up your valuables, or move them to another location, (such as a relative's house) until the work is completed. Hide your liquor, medication, firearms and minor appliances too. These are often a temptation to thieves.

LIGHTING YOUR HOME

Denying a possible intruder the cover of darkness is a principal advantage of home lighting. Lights can prevent a possible crime or break-in on your property. A criminal is not likely to force his way into your home if his actions are highly visible. Most homes and apartment buildings have lights positioned at their entrances. If your dwelling is isolated, the brighter the light the better.

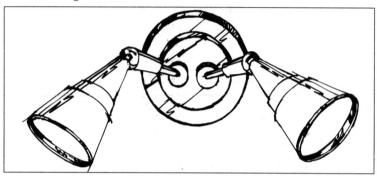

Consider positioning spot-lights to properly illuminate the sides and win-dows of your home as well as the entrances and driveways.

If your home or apartment has a lot of trees or shrubs, these areas should also be illuminated. In most cases, at least one or more of a home's windows are hidden from the view of the street and surrounding homes. These are areas of vulnerability which also require lighting.

When you retire for the evening, do not turn off the interior lights. Leave a front-room light on all night. If an intruder can see from the street that your exterior and interior lights are on, this will serve as a deterrent. In most cases, a would-be burglar will seek out a place that is poorly lit, rather than attempt to gain entry at the risk of being observed.

YOUR DOG

Throughout civilized history, dogs have been used to guard lives, property, locate criminals, contraband and/or children.

Although not all dogs will actually attack an intruder, the psychological advantage they provide is invaluable. Very few intruders will attempt a crime once they are aware of a dog's presence. A dog in the home, or outside, guarding the property, will help prevent intrusion.

NEIGHBORHOOD WATCH

One of the most effective methods of crime prevention is a simple, common sense approach. Police can't be everywhere at all times. Half of all home burglaries occur during the day when alert neighbors could spot suspicious activity and report it. In many communities, concerned citizens are involved in a neighborhood watch, block watch, or citizen crime watch. The common goal of these groups is simply: neighbors watching out for one another. Check with the local police to see if your community has such a program. If so, join it. If not, why not start one?

HOME SECURITY CHECKLIST

A. Safety tips when you're home:

1. Always keep all doors locked.
2. Know who is at the door before opening it.
3. If a stranger is persistent on the phone, do not reveal you are alone. Hang up.
4. Call the police if you hear noises outside the house i.e., prowlers.

B. When you go on vacation:

1. Make your house look lived in.
2. Notify the police and your neighbors.
3. Stop mail, newspapers and any other deliveries to your home.
4. Be sure to set a timer switch for inside and outside door lights.
5. Make the outside of your house look lived in: cut grass, shovel snow, and, if possible, keep cars in driveways.
6. Arrange to have your dog fed and walked at home rather than kept at a kennel. If you don't have a dog, having someone you trust water your plants serves the same purpose of having your home look "lived in!"
7. Arrange for garbage and trash to be put out and picked up as usual.
8. Arrange for secure storage of furs, jewelry and other valuables outside your house while you are away.
9. Have alarm system checked before leaving.
10. Avoid publicity about your pending trip.
11. Do not pack your car the night before departure; load it quickly in the morning.
12. Before leaving, check to see that all doors and windows are locked.

C. Instructions to leave for a babysitter:

1. Do not let friends visit.
2. Here are important phone numbers:
   a. *Where I can be reached:*
   b. *Children's doctor:*
   c. *Fire:*
   d. *Poison control center:*
3. Never reveal that adults are not at home.
4. Call police if you hear noises around the house.
5. Keep doors and lower-level windows locked at night.
6. If a stranger calls on the phone, hang up immediately. If he/she calls, again contact the police and me.
7. Use good judgement when opening doors. Don't let anyone in unless you know him/her. If it's a friend of yours tell him/her you're not allowed to have company while babysitting.

D. Strangers (utility workers or service employees) enter your home:

1. Check the business identification of the person. If it's the electric or phone company or a cleaning service, he/she should have a photo ID Call the company before letting him/her in if you have any doubt.
2. Do not leave valuables in sight.
3. Do not reveal that you live alone.
4. If possible, have someone else there to greet the stranger besides yourself.
5. Do not let a stranger enter your house if you are alone.

E. General tips for home security:

1. If you walk in on a burglar, do not fight him. Do as you are told and report the incident as soon as possible.
2. Make arrangements with your neighbors to keep an eye on each other. If a stranger is at your door, your neighbor can keep him/her under observation. If he/she breaks in, your neighbor can call the police.
3. Be certain that all outside doors are protected by a proper locking device. Dead-bolt locks are best. Doors should be of solid construction and should fit snugly in their door frame.
4. All windows should be properly protected by a window lock. Added security can be obtained by the use of a nail in a pre-drilled hole.
5. Do not leave keys in a hiding place. Burglars always look around for "hidden" keys before attempting to break in. Any hidden place you think of has been used before, and a professional criminal knows it!
6. Basement windows should be protected by bars or with heavy plastic sheeting.
7. Install a "peephole" in all outside doors. Intercoms are helpful for an added sense of security.
8. Dogs are a deterrent to any would-be intruder. If you have an attack dog be sure that it is well trained and under complete control at all times. A loose attack dog can hurt innocent people.
9. Police recommend marking all your appliances with an electric scriber on hidden locations (for future ID). Some police departments give decals for windows stating that the premises have been scribed.
10. If you find your home has been broken into, leave everything alone and report the burglary to the police. The thief may have left clues behind that could lead to an arrest.
11. Have alarms installed by reputable dealers. Units must be properly placed and controlled.
12. Always have keys ready to open doors, especially when arriving home late.

HOME SECURITY CHECKLIST

13. Keep outside lights on a timer so that the entrance to your home is always well illuminated.
14. Women should always conceal the fact that they are living in their home alone. Mailboxes should be addressed with initials rather than "Miss."
15. Keep night chains on doors for added protection.
16. Secure any glass in the immediate vicinity of door knobs and lock doors.
17. If you lose your keys, replace your locks immediately.
18. Do not reveal personal information to strangers on the phone.
19. Hedges, shrubs, fences and trees should not block visibility from street to windows.
20. Light the exterior of houses very well, and on all sides.
21. Light all gates and fences surrounding your property.
22. Illuminate all shadowed areas caused by trees, shrubbery or the house, especially around doors and windows.

F. General tips for apartment dwellers' security:

1. When moving into an apartment, look for these security oriented features:
   a. Doormen or security guards to screen visitors.
   b. Attended elevators.
   c. Properly secured interior and exterior fire stairwells.
   d. Properly secured garages.
   e. Remotely operated door-opening systems, with intercom systems and closed-circuit T.V.
   f. Interior-view mirrors in self-secured elevators.
   g. Adequate lighting.
   h. Protection against alcoves or other blind spots being used as hiding places.
   i. Roof doors operable only from inside.
2. Change locks immediately after moving into your apartment.
3. Protect "spare" or emergency keys.
4. Equip outside doors with chain locks and peepholes.
5. Do not indicate your gender on a mailbox or doorplate.
6. Protect windows. Those adjoining fire escapes should prevent illegal entry but not prohibit emergency exit.
7. Know you neighbors and work together for mutual security.
8. Report anything peculiar such as faulty equipment or an unusual accident.
9. Do not admit anyone to the building with your remote door opener unless you know the person and purpose of the visit.
10. Seek company on trips to a laundry room.

HOME SECURITY CHECKLIST

11. Do not ride self-service elevators with suspicious looking strangers.
12. Use the emergency button if threatened in an elevator.
13. Alert the management, police and neighbors of the presence of unauthorized persons.

Potential Danger In Your Work Environment

LEAVING YOUR HOME

Have your mace key defender handy, just in case, You are attacked.

The daily routine we know as "going to work" generally takes about one-third of each day. Since we spend such a great deal of time out of the house, it is a good idea to recognize the potential vulnerabilities that going to work encompasses. We often don't place importance on our routines. We don't think about them once they are established. This is a mistake because anyone who can familiarize him or herself with your routines can know our vulnerabilities better than you know them yourself. In essence, this is how the hunter operates in the wild. He stalks his prey according to his prey's habits. Once the hunter knows his prey's habits traveling to and from his lair, his habitual movements, eating habits, etc., the prey does not stand a chance. To assure success the hunter will often study his prey's activities for days before striking.

In our modern day "Concrete Jungle," we, as potential prey for criminals, do not always have the ability to alter our routines. We cannot change our work habits simply for security's sake. We risk losing our jobs. However, there are many things you can do to ensure your safety while you are out of your home each day. First of all be aware. Learn to view your life and routines objectively, from an outsider's point of view. Once you accomplish this, you can identify areas of personal vulnerability and take steps to rectify them.

When you leave your home, first make sure that all windows and doors are securely locked. Turn off or unplug all appliances and leave a light on if you return home after dark. It might be worth your while to invest in a timer that will turn the lights on automatically at dusk. This is cheaper than leaving the lights on all day long, and gives your home the appearance of being occupied during the day. After all, you would not have the light on if you were home before dusk.

YOUR CAR

There are several ways to enhance your safety in and around your car. Obviously, having a private garage with a remote garage door opener is ideal. This allows you to safely enter and exit your car without stepping foot outside. If you must park on the street or in public lots, try to choose a non-secluded location. If necessary, get together with fellow tenants and request proper lighting and an alarm system. You might also consider carpooling. Not only is this economical, it's safe.

However, if all this is not possible, there are common sense, street-wise safety steps you should follow. Before entering your car, look inside to ensure it is unoccupied. If you clearly recall locking the doors, and they now appear to be unlocked, step away, do not enter the car and call the police. Once you have safely entered your car, lock all the doors and roll the windows up. Be sure to fuel your car the night before so your gas tank is at least half full.

All cars should be equipped with these items for safety's sake:

1. Spare tire and tire changing tools including a jack and tire-iron
2. Fire extinguisher
3. First aid kit
4. Flares
5. White flag
6. Blanket (in case you get stuck in the cold)
7. Additional repair tools (depending on your ability)

If for some reason you have car trouble, or you break down on the way to work, there are steps you should follow. First, pull off the road away from traffic. Raise the hood of your car and tie a white flag on your antenna. Then get back into your car, lock the doors and await police help. Keep the vehicle in park with your emergency brake on and the engine off. If another motorist offers help, the safest course is to roll your window down slightly and request they call emergency road service, the police or a family member.

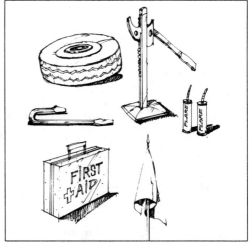

Make sure your car is equipped for safety.

It is wise not to exit the car if possible. If you must change a tire, first put the emergency brake on, then block the tires so that the car will not roll off the jack and cause bodily harm or damage to your car. Be sure not to lock your keys in the trunk or in the car.

If you are driving to work and another driver attempts to harass you in any way, do not respond with arguments, obscene gestures, etc. Write down their license plate number, car make and model and continue on your way. Later you can report the incident to the police. Finally, don't pick up hitchhikers!

SAFETY IN A PARKING LOT

When you arrive at your destination, study the environment for a moment before exiting your car. Identify any potentially dangerous areas. Is anyone present in the parking lot? Outdoor parking lots offer little or no place for someone to hide. But indoor parking lots do, even if the parking lot is in the building where you work. Are there any areas where someone could hide? Make a mental note of any possibility, thus preparing yourself for any circumstance. I don't wish to encourage fear or paranoia, simply awareness of your environment. Keep your mace, keys or a similar weapon of defense in your hand as you pass through the garage or parking lot on your way to the elevator or stairwell, etc., ready for immediate use. In a later chapter I will discuss how to make use of such defense weapons effectively.

Whenever possible, try to walk with other people, even if you have to ask someone to escort you, especially at night. Assume an air of confidence as you walk. Consider carrying a cane or umbrella to and from the car as these can be formidable weapons, and present an intimidating image to help discourage would-be assailants. You might also want to carry an airhorn or whistle to blow an alarm if you are attacked. Even screaming will often scare off an attacker.

ELEVATORS

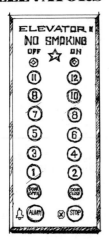

Use discretion when riding an elevator with a stranger. If someone entered the elevator who makes you feel uneasy, trust your instincts and get out of the elevator immediately. Make sure you study the elevator's operation buttons. If you are attacked, push the "ALARM" or the "STOP" button. Many elevators are equipped with an intercom system which engages when the emergency stop button is used. Remain calm so you can report your location, direction, etc. to whomever is listening. Later we will cover techniques which enable you to defend yourself in such situations. Finally, avoid walking in stairways alone. They are a common locale for criminal activity.

PUBLIC TRANSPORTATION

Many people, especially those who live near or within major cities, use a public transportation system each day. Not all public transportation systems have security or police protection. Those that do employ enough personnel to afford you an immediate response to any criminal activity. When using public transportation, awareness is the key to self-defense.

BUSES

Buses afford moderate safety because you usually are among many riders. Refrain from riding alone if possible, and never leave any package or briefcase unattended. Keep all your possessions firmly in hand while waiting for a bus, after entering and while exiting the bus. Never exit a bus in unfamiliar territory. Your wait for the next bus could be of an undetermined duration, perhaps hours, and could strand you in a potentially dangerous environment. If you are lost, the bus driver will afford you any assistance he or she can render, or you can remain on the bus until you feel safe. While you're riding, keep all your possessions in plain sight on your lap or in your hands, thus discouraging pickpockets. As you exit the bus remain alert for any would-be purse snatchers (or other assailants) waiting for victims as they get off.

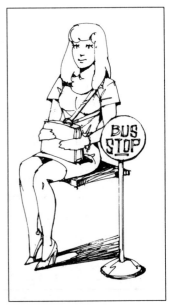

Keep all your possessions firmly in hand while waiting for a bus.

Always check to see if your taxi is legitimate.

TAXICABS

When hailing a taxi, be sure it is a legitimate one. Never enter a taxi with a questionable or suspicious appearance. Having entered, scan the taxi for the usual equipment such as the meter, maps, charts or change box. If these are not present, exit immediately. If you decide to ride, provide clear-cut instructions. If the driver does not follow them, create any excuse to exit, such as waiting for a red light or stop sign. Make a note of the license plate number, taxi number, the driver's license number and a description of the driver and vehicle. Notify the police and taxi service.

SUBWAYS AND TRAINS

Subways and trains often present a potentially dangerous environment. Never travel alone if you have a choice. Never ride subways at night, if you can avoid it, or sit alone in a subway car. If possible, sit with others near the front of the train. If there are any guards, sit near them, or near the driver. If any subway rider(s) act in a belligerent or threatening manner, move to a more populated subway car if possible. If not, remain calm and confident. Have your mace key defender handy, just in case. When exiting the subway car, move quickly through the turnstile and exit the station. Do not loiter in the subway station and try to stay near others who are also leaving.

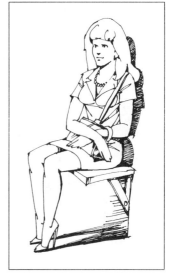

Hold your valuables close to your body.

TRAVELING BY AIR

Although most airports provide an ample degree of safety and security, a few simple procedures merit mentioning. Make sure to confirm your flight and leave your itinerary with a friend or relative. Be sure to lock all your baggage after writing your name, address and phone number both on the inside and also on a tag. Remove previous flight tags and stickers from your baggage to prevent any misrouting of your possessions. Don't leave your carry-on bags unattended, even for a minute. Don't use airport lockers; they can be broken into. Finally, if you are traveling with children, always keep them within eyesight. If a child must use a public restroom, accompany the child and bring other children with you. Do not split up the group if you can avoid doing so.

SEXUAL HARASSMENT

The term "sexual harassment" encompasses a wide range of behavior on the part of the aggressor as well as the victim. Victims of sexual harassment are often unaware of their rights, or that harassment is occurring. What constitutes sexual harassment is determined by many factors, the greatest of which is the feeling of being harassed, coerced, or embarrassed by sexually oriented behavior on the part of an aggressor. Although the emotional response to sexual harassment will vary depending on the individual, the reaction to sexual harassment is usually determined by an individual's sense of self-esteem and self-confidence. It is often a victim's behavior that triggers the aggressive behavior on the part of the sexual harasser. An

Don't be a victim of Sexual Harassment, report it to the Better Business Bureau.

aggressor can sense vulnerable personality types and is drawn to them. Do not allow yourself to be intimidated under any circumstances.

You have every right to report any behavior with sexual undertones that makes you feel uncomfortable to the proper authority. Job discrimination and job security are often linked to the sexual advances by individuals with authority over an attractive employee. This is illegal. Do not allow yourself to be a victim of this. Report the harassment to the human resources department where you work, an agency like the Better Business Bureau, your attorney, or the president of the company. Be aware of your rights, of what course of action is available to you, and take action!

This, refers to verbal sexual harassment or intimidation, or minor physical advances. Actual physical assault and rape are covered later in this book, and I will discuss basic streetwise self-defense techniques for such situations.

WORK ENVIRONMENT CHECKLIST

A. Public transportation (buses, taxies, subways, trains):

1. Do not fall asleep on any of the above modes of transportation; stay awake and alert at all times.
2. Keep all valuables in front of you.
3. Distribute valuables among several pockets. That way if someone tries to rob you, you may have to surrender valuables in one pocket.
4. Keep a distance from the path of oncoming transportation.
5. Do not let someone stand directly behind you when waiting for transportation, they could easily push you in the path of a vehicle.
6. When waiting for transportation, try to mingle within the crowd; a lone traveler is an easy target.
7. When carrying valuables, (pocketbooks, briefcase, camera, case) keep them close to you (on your legs or in your hands). Do not place them down on the seat.
8. Do not flash a lot of money when paying for a fare or ticket.
9. Stay in a well-lit area. Do not wait in dark areas.
10. Never board an empty subway car. Always try to board the central area of transportation. Most people get on and remain there (trains, subways).
11. Make the most use out of public transportation. Minimize your walking distance.
12. Do not use public transportation if you have been drinking or are ill. You will become a ready target in a danger zone.
13. When getting off public transportation, always take note of your environment and the people in it.
14. Bathrooms in public transportation terminals are very dangerous. Be aware of surroundings when using these facilities.

B. Private transportation (cars):

1. Have keys ready before heading to a car.
2. Be aware of your surroundings while walking to your car. Make sure that no one is following you.
3. As you approach your car, check underneath it.
4. Check back seat before getting into vehicle.
5. Keep all doors locked.
6. Keep windows 3/4 way up when stopped at a traffic light.

7. If you left your car in good condition and it does not start when you come back, be suspicious immediately.
   a. Do not accept unsolicited offers of assistance.
   b. Do not unlock the door to admit a stranger.

8. Avoid driving your vehicle through areas that you know are crime infested

9. If you see a motorist who needs assistance, drive to a phone and send help. Do not stop.

10. Do not get out of your car in a dark, remote location, even if you have been involved in a car accident. Drive to an open service station or business and call the police. The accident may have been deliberate.

11. If your car breaks down, unlock the hood and raise it. Get back into the car and try to have someone call the police.

12. When valet parking, take your house keys off your key ring. Also, remove any other valuables or papers which may indicate home address.

13. Do not display accessories such as tape players or CB radios where they will attract a thief's attention.

14. If, while you are driving, and you believe someone is following you—

   DO NOT...

   a. Pull off to the side of the road to see if the person will pass.

   b. Travel down side streets.

   c. Go home.

   DO...

   a. Pull into a well-lit gas station or store and see if the other person also pulls in or goes away.

   b. Stay on well-lit heavily traveled streets.

   c. Keep windows rolled up and doors locked.

   d. Slow down your pace so you are observed by other vehicles. Beep your horn if necessary.

   e. Drive directly to a police station, fire station or hospital emergency room.

   f. If the follower panics and speeds past your car, be sure to get his/her license number.

15. If someone attempts to enter your car at a stoplight or stop sign, drive away, sounding your horn, even if it means running a red light. In general, turn to the right when driving away.

C. Street security (walking, jogging and bike riding):

1. Do not carry more money or valuables than you can afford to lose.

2. If approached by a robber, cooperate. Surrender your valuables. They are worth less than you are.

3. If the robber attempts to physically harm you, defend yourself.

4. Walk on the side of the street facing oncoming traffic.

5. On a busy street, carry your purse or briefcase on the side farthest from the curb.

6. Carry a shoulder strap purse so that it hangs straight down from your shoulder, suspended between your arm and body. The strap should not cross your body.
7. Carry handbags with a short strap as you would a football, with your hand placed through the strap, clutching the bag.
8. If you are being followed on a well-traveled street, indicate to your pursuer that you are aware of him by: slowing down, speeding up, or reversing directions. Then go straight for help.
9. If followed on a deserted street, walk briskly to a well-lit and populated area. Do not run straight for home unless help is available there.
10. Running, screaming and the use of a loud whistle are recommended defensive weapons. But do not keep whistles around your neck.
11. If you must carry large amounts of money, do not keep it all in one place.
12. Do not carry keys in the same place as identification that would tell a robber where to find the door the key fits into.
13. Avoid walking the streets alone after dark. Use a taxi whenever practical.
14. If you must walk alone at night, do not walk near cars parked at the curb, or close to doorways or shrubbery which could conceal a mugger.
15. If necessary, do not hesitate to walk in the street.
16. If you must walk streets at night regularly, vary your routine to minimize the possibility of someone lying in wait to assault you.

Potential Danger In Shopping Malls

Shopping malls, as with all other locations, present a set of unique circumstances for which certain precautions must be taken. While your personal safety is hardly at risk when in the act of shopping, this does not include traveling to and from the mall, or across the parking lot to your car.

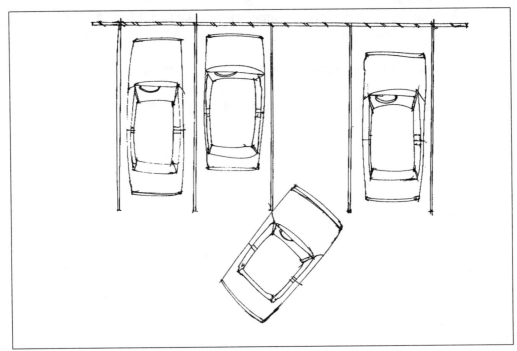

PARK YOUR CAR IN CROWDED AREAS

Don't take anything for granted, don't park your car to far from the mall, or in a secluded area. If you work in the mall, consider the fact that the parking lot won't be as crowded later at night when you leave from work. Although many crimes are committed in broad daylight, a lot of illegal

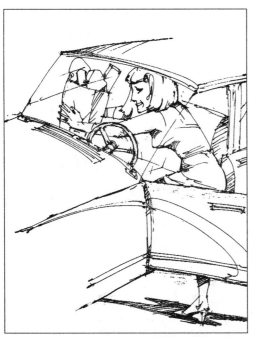

activity in mall parking lots occurs at night. These crimes range from purse snatching to kidnapping, from mugging or car theft, to rape or kidnapping.

Use the same security procedures as in any other potentially dangerous situation. When you pull into the mall parking lot, make sure your car doors are still locked. You should have locked them after you entered your car. As you pull into the lot consider all the factors of safety, and choose your parking space accordingly. If you work at the mall, leave home early enough to allow yourself ample time to choose a good spot. This might take a few minutes. Don't be in such a rush to park that you take the first parking space available. Wait for a good spot, if possible. After parking your car, gather all necessary belongings in one hand, your keys firmly grasped in the other hand. Make sure before exiting your car that the lights are off, and the emergency brake on. Unlock only the door you are using to exit. Leave the car and glance all around you, taking in a 360 degree view.

If no one is near, lock the car, door and begin to walk quickly towards the mall entrance. Avoid walking near cars if possible because cars provide cover where a would-be assailant might be hiding.

If, after stepping out of your car, you notice someone you didn't see as you parked the car suddenly nearby, get back into you, car immediately, and lock your door. Stay in the car and see if he/she is just another shopper heading towards the mall. If they remain around you, you are safe inside your car. Simply start the car and drive away. Report this event to the police, giving a description of the individual(s) if possible. Many crimes in shopping mall parking lots occur when a person first exits or enters his/ her car. Robbers, muggers and even rapists are known to jump in the car's passenger side door and threaten drivers with weapons. If you remember to keep all car doors locked at all times, you can help prevent this from happening to you.

When returning to your car, there are several safety measures you can employ. You might consider having your packages delivered. If you aren't burdened with packages, your hands are free for defense and you become a less likely target for thieves. Keep your purse or briefcase firmly grasped in one hand, your keys in the other. Make sure your mace or other hand-held defensive weapon is close at hand.

As you approach your car, do so cautiously, scanning the immediate surroundings. It's always wise to park under or near a street light to illuminate your car at night, and to discourage criminals. Approach your car from the rear, and if possible, look in between the nearby cars to make sure you are alone. Once you determine that no one is hiding behind a nearby car, look underneath your car and the cars next to yours on either side. A desperate person will take desperate measures, including hiding underneath the next car or your car, grabbing or slashing your legs as you open your car door to enter, and thus gaining immediate control of the situation. Enter your car quickly, placing your packages on the car seat next to you. This saves valuable time spent opening your trunk to load packages and exposing yourself to a potentially dangerous situation. If you must carry packages out to your car, consider either driving your car to the service entrance and loading packages there, or having someone from the store help you by carrying your packages and escorting you to the car. Once your packages are secured, make sure all car doors are locked and drive home.

If you feel threatened in any way, scream, use your whistle, and if you have to use your hand-held defensive weapon as I'll describe later! There are many new personal defense weapons available on the market and some of them even attach to your keychain. A whistle or air horn are also good for sounding an alarm. If these aren't handy, a good loud scream can ward off many would-be attackers.

Potential Danger In Recreational Environments

Although traveling and vacationing provide many with a source of relaxation and recreation, criminals succeed in ruining many a vacation or trip by exploiting the vulnerabilities of the traveler. Unfortunately, what is concieved as an escape from our daily troubles can end up as a source of even greater difficulty, or even as a disaster.

Such scenarios can often be avoided by observing a few common sense precautions. I will advise you of precautionary measures that will allow you to implement whatever course of action the situation warrants. Again, the key to survival is awareness. Even on vacations or trips, identify vulnerabilities and implement precautionary measures.

When you travel, you represent an easy target to the criminal. You are outside your normal environment, possibly in unfamiliar territory. You are isolated from friends and conventional support conveniences. Often entranced with the stimuli of the vacation or vacation area, your guard is down. Your manner of dress, speech and actions identify you as a stranger to the environment because you are out of your element. While traveling, you may be tempted to carry large amounts of cash. You may suffer from jet lag, you may drink more, dine out, and generally do everything but keep a low profile and blend into the surroundings.

DATING

Provocative dress can attract trouble. Overly aggressive males often view see-through blouses or short skirts as an invitation for them to display their would-be dominance. This isn't to say you shouldn't dress as you wish, just that some unpleasant situations could be avoided by your being aware of the image you project.

Would-be attackers observe the dress of their intended victim for vulnerabilities. In the case of a physical assault tight, constricting clothing and high heels make it very difficult for you to run or fight. The intentions of a friendly man are often sufficiently shielded from a woman's intuition to mask the dark side of his nature. Don't place yourself in jeopardy. If you meet a man while you are on a trip or vacation, (or even in your hometown) and want to know him better, be cautious. On your first date, never agree to go someplace where the two of you will be alone. Take separate cars. Get to know the man in a public place first. Then make your decision. If you feel you don't know the man well enough, trust your instincts. Any man worth having will not be offended or discouraged simply because you are exercising a little streetwise common sense. In fact, it's a good idea to exercise caution when you meet a man in your home territory as well. Date rape in which the victim already knows her attacker is common.

Above all, when on vacation or out of your home territory, don't display your valuables. An assailant is likely to pass you by in favor of someone who looks affluent, with expensive clothes and flashy jewelry. In terms of crime prevention, looking average and keeping a low profile is a wise precaution.

PURSE SNATCHING

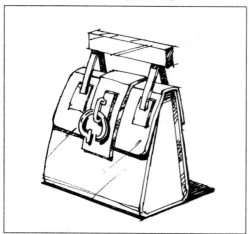

A Strong purse is important to travel with.

Selecting an appropriate purse is also important. Pick one with a strong, well-attached handle, and a sturdy mechanical catch that must be manually disengaged before opening. Try to avoid purses with a magnetic clasp, spring closure and especially open-top bags. Be aware that criminals are well acquainted with various types of purses and prefer those that offer the least resistance. Don't make it easy for an attacker. Make snatching your purse as difficult as possible. One of the best methods is to have the purse handle around your arm, held by the arm to your chest. This body language indicates you're aware of your bag and makes it physically difficult to snatch the purse. In addition, beware of strange or unknown women in washrooms. A restroom can be quite profitable for female purse snatchers. Never keep all your money, traveler's checks or credit cards in one purse, always leave some behind, locked in a safe-deposit box or in your room in case of an emergency. Many hotels offer safe-deposit boxes as a convenience for their guests.

PLANNING YOUR TRIP

Whether you will be traveling alone or with your family, you should assemble a careful, organized, and complete priority checklist well in advance of your vacation. The loss, misplacement or forgetting of an object or possession could be avoided this way. If you are planning a family trip, gather the family together for the creation of your priority checklist. By taking the time to arrange priorities, and by using the input of all family members, almost all details can be worked out with all sharing in the responsibilities.

Discuss the entire vacation from beginning to end, covering all possible scenarios. Discuss possible hazards, dangers and precautionary measures. To simply give your children general directions like "stay close to me," or "avoid strangers" is not good enough. By discussing details of your trip, as well as possible hazardous scenarios, you are promoting responsibility, involvement, awareness and safety within your family unit. Allow your children to contribute. By encouraging children to become aware of what could happen in various scenarios, you start them on the road to individual awareness of possible danger.

PRECAUTIONARY MEASURES

HOME SECURITY WHILE ON VACATION

Too many homes are the target of vandals and thieves while the home owner is on vacation. An empty home is too enticing a target for a thief. A home that appears occupied, or at least attended by someone, presents a discouraging target for a thief, vandal or burglar. Before departing for your trip you should first inform local police, your landlord, friends and family members of your trip and request that they keep a watchful eye on your home in your absence. Leave your home key with someone you trust, asking friends and family to report any suspicious activity to the police. Stop all newspapers and mail deliveries, or arrange to have the deliveries picked up by someone in your absence. If gone for more than a week, you might consider having the lawn cut, or, in winter, having the snow removed from your driveway and walk. Make sure a friend, neighbor or family member leaves trash in your trash can for regular pick up, giving the home the appearance of occupation. If you can leave a vehicle parked in your regular driveway spot, do so. Leave all window blinds and shades in their normal position. If you don't have a timer on your home lighting, make sure someone can turn on both the inside and outside lights of your home. Don't discuss your plans for a vacation or trip with anyone, especially in casual conversation or in a public locale, except with highly trusted friends or relatives. Never leave notes on any doors saying you are away or out for the day.

FAMILY IDENTIFICATION

If you are planning a family trip or vacation, be sure to supply each family member with some form of personal identification. Usually parents make sure their children never leave their side, but what would you do if your child somehow got separated from you? An identification card can be made for your children and encased in plastic, often pinned to an article of clothing. This identification card should include pertinent information such as blood type, allergies, medication or health problems, in addition to the address and phone number of your current accommodations. In addition to this card, a daily family itinerary card should be carried on each child's person. This would contain temporary information such as vehicle ID, where the family is, and their itinerary for the day.

Mark your luggage with complete identification and always lock it.

Give your children their personal ID card and itinerary, and then instruct them about what they must do if they get separated from you. Tell them to look for a policeman, security guard or similar official if possible. If at a park, tell them not to leave the park alone under any circumstances. Make sure everyone understands the activities planned and the time schedule for the activities. This way, each knows the others' location if separated. Each family member should make an effort to remember what type of clothes the others are wearing. Never split up the group leaving one child alone. Each parent must assume responsibility for one half of the group. Inform others when your're going to to use a restroom, and leave your purse with the other family members. Hold all purses and cameras securely. Do not leave them unattended. It's not a bad idea to locate and identify a policeman or security person, and point him/her, to your children, in case of emergency.

If you are planning an extended trip by car, consider additional safety tips. First, have your car checked out by a reputable mechanic to assure that it can safely make the trip. This includes checking tires, brakes, all hoses, fan belt, the battery and all fluids. It might be a good idea to join Triple A (AAA) or another reputable auto club for the convenience of 24-hour emergency road service. Avoid driving long distances without periodic breaks. Try to drive during the daylight hours if you are traveling long distances, and try to keep your gas tank as full as possible. This will enable you to reach large towns with open gas stations. If you are traveling on busy highways, convenient rest stops, gas stations and even restaurants are available for your use.

Pick up your luggage in the claim area immediately.

If you must drive at night, avoid short cuts and deserted back roads. Avoid hanging clothes in the back seat. Use your trunk if possible because clothes hanging in the back seat indicate you are traveling. Keep cameras and other valuables out of sight. Finally, make sure you have proper road maps, a spare tire, several flashlights, a dependable jack and flares to help ensure your safety.

If you or your family are planning to travel by air, bus or any other public carrier, there are several common sense, streetwise precautionary measures to consider. If traveling by bus or train, get a map of your route so you can understanding your travel route, stops and transfers.

Realize that bus and subway terminals are frequented by criminals in search of likely victims. Try to plan your trip, avoiding long waits in these dangerous areas. Stay in crowded, well-lit areas, in view of uniformed employees and beware of strangers asking for directions.

When seated, keep your purse in your lap, not on the floor or the next seat. Be aware of the people around you. If someone acts suspicious or threatening, inform an official. If traveling by subway, be sure to stay a safe distance from the edge of the platform. The subway platform is a favorite location for purse snatchers and muggers. Stay alert at all times. Remember that the criminal always chooses the victim according to vulnerability. Don't present the image of an easy target, and you will most likely be left alone.

Make sure your baggage is locked and marked with complete identification on both the inside and outside. Remove all old tags. Never leave carry-on luggage unattended. Insure your valuables and credit cards, and avoid carrying large sums of cash. The most likely time to lose your baggage is before it's checked in, and after unloading the bus, train or plane.

Try to keep your baggage in sight as much as possible. When you arrive at your destination, go directly to the baggage claim area and pick up your luggage and other baggage. This could help prevent your belongings from being stolen.

VACATION SECURITY

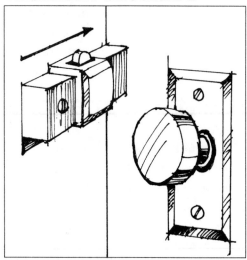

Portable travel locks are available on the market today.

When staying out of state, remember you are in unfamiliar territory. Your vehicle license plate identifies you as a stranger, making you a prime target for the local criminal. This criminal also realizes you probably won't stay long, not long enough to report a missing camera or similar item to the local authorities. Unfortunately, the room key you are issued when checking in isn't the only key that opens your door. Other copies exist. In addition, most hotel room locks can be opened with a credit card or spatula.

Unless the hotel doors supply additional locks, such as a dead-bolt, door chain and door viewer, you might consider improvising certain protective measures of your own.

For example, a chair wedged with the back of the chair against the door knob is an effective safety precaution while you are in your room. A simple rubber door-wedge can be inserted under the door, effectively preventing the door from being opened from either side. Purchased at any hardware store, these provide practical, economical, portable safety. There are a variety of portable travel locks available on the market today. When used, the door cannot be opened unless broken down. It's up to you to decide what you require for peace of mind while away from home.

Preventing Domestic Violence

Potentially dangerous situations outside the home are many. But most of us are lucky enough to feel safe in our homes. For a child reared in a happy home, the home represents a safe haven, a place of warmth, love and security. For an abused child, the home becomes a prison; the child's life becomes a nightmare.

One unfortunate repercussion of abuse in the home is often criminal behavior. This isn't to say that all of today's battered children are tomorrow's criminals. Yet there is something to be said for the correlation between domestic violence and crime. Not only is the initial act of child abuse a crime, with repetition over years, the hostility and anti-social tendencies displayed to the child become ingrained, part of the child's nature. It is both unrealistic and irresponsible to think that constant, severe beatings, or even continual verbal berating won't take an emotional toll on any child, manifesting itself in some way later in life.

CHILD ABUSE

Statistics show that many criminals who commit violent crimes were victims of some kind of abuse earlier in their lives. Thus, the acts of child abuse in the home eventually affect all of us in one way or another. If one family's domestic violence brings repercussions to another family years later (potentially with the loss of a life), obviously the issue of child abuse and the need for prevention concern everyone. Domestic violence is a more sociological problem than previously believed. And even though domestic violence is not a new problem, recent increases in reports bring greater awareness of the extent of domestic violence due to media exposure.

In years past, neighbors and other well-intentioned persons refrained from reporting child abuse. One reason was fear of legal retaliation. Please realize that no one can be prosecuted for acting in good faith when someone's safety is concerned. There are laws requiring law enforcement officials, teachers, social workers and day care providers to report all or any signs of domestic violence. The specifics of what legally constitutes abuse are determined by individual states. If you ever suspect the abuse of a child, choose to err on the side of caution. Call the local child advocacy office. Child abuse can be defined as the continued abuse or neglect of the child by the child's legal guardian.

Another reason why people fail to report domestic violence is due to ignorance, lack of exposure and unawareness of the problem. Legal standards are established in the court system when a precedence is established. Having seen the causes and effects of domestic violence on the daily news, it is easier for all of us to identify similar or possible signs pointing to abuse of some kind.

Child abuse occurs for many different reasons. Perhaps a parent is under great stress due to financial burdens. Feeling badly about the inability to meet financial obligations can cause frustration, anger and abusive behavior. An unhappy marriage is often the case. Perhaps one or both partners experience a great deal of stress due to a lack of harmony between them, causing verbal or physical conflict. Not only is this a poor example for the children, hostility between parents can easily turn and focus on children.

Another cause of child abuse is drug or alcohol abuse. The inability to deal with life's problems is self-evident in the drug or alcohol abuser, and his or her lack of self-control and common sense is obvious. If you know any parent who is a drug or alcohol abuser, and you notice signs of child abuse or neglect, don't be afraid to report it.

Child abuse is not confined to the home environment. The school, work and play environment of a child could also be the source of possible child abuse.

PHYSICAL ABUSE

The term "physical abuse" first brings continued or unwarranted beatings to mind first. Courts do not convict parents for slapping a child's hand or disciplining a child for bad behavior. Therefore discipline becomes abuse when it is continual and unwarranted. Bruises, black and blue marks, discoloration of the eyes, bloody noses or lips are often a sign of possible child abuse.

I don't suggest you interfere in your neighbor's privacy at the first sign of injury. Some energetic children have been known to be accident prone. Skinned knees or hands, bruises on the lower leg or scratches may not be indications of abuse. Black and blue marks, swollen eyes or mouths, injured wrists or marks on the upper body may be an indication of child abuse. Remain keenly aware and report suspected abuse if your instincts tell you someone is in jeopardy.

Another form of physical child abuse is neglect: the deprivation of needs such as proper food, water and general nutrition. Even more extreme is the lack of shelter or clothing. Depriving a child of a late snack as a form of discipline, or simply failing to cater to a spoiled child is a far cry from a pattern of continually sending a child to bed without dinner as a punishment, or failing to provide enough food. Some forms of child abuse are intentional and others are unintentional. The result is the same: physical and emotional injury or death.

If the parents fail or refuse to recognize a problem, even if the parents themselves aren't the cause, what recourse does an abused child have? It is important that all children are taught about the possibility of abuse, the punishment for it, and the importance of reporting any abuse (their own or a friend's) *immediately*. Enrolling your child in a self-defense school or martial arts dojo (school) is a way for your child to learn defensive tactics. The awareness of possible abuse combined with the ability to defend him/herself gives your child a margin of safety that can make a difference.

Naturally a child cannot hope to beat an adult attack into submission. However, all adults have vulnerable areas of the body and children can deliver blows there if necessary. Strikes to the eyes, throat, nose or groin can definitely put an attacker at a severe disadvantage. Once the attacker is stunned, the child can hopefully escape and report the crime to the proper authority or his/her parents.

In the case of domestic abuse, often a relative, neighbor or friend files the report.

EMOTIONAL ABUSE

Emotional abuse ranges from obvious and extreme insults and degradations to more subtle forms. Emotional abuse often results from a parent's lack of interest in the child's life, performance at school or relationships. This type of parent spends as little time with his/her children as possible, and has little or no interest in being a proper role model. Much of what children absorb in the home in the areas of emotional health and behavior is learned by example. Parents may have to work long hours, never having time to spend with children, unable to teach them anything. The children may not suffer immediately, but will manifest problems later in life: inability to communicate, anti-social behavior, or lack of morals, no sense of right and wrong.

SPOUSE ABUSE

Similar to child abuse, spouse abuse has received more media attention recently. It is estimated that one in seven women is the victim of spouse abuse. Women rarely report abuse at the hands of their husband, feeling guilty, afraid, embarrassed, inadequate as a wife or mother, or simply that it is a private matter. In some cases, religious considerations or fear of divorce or family break-up prevent a woman from reporting.

Spouse abuse tends to occur more during vacations or the holidays. Besides the stress the holidays bring, spouses are together more frequently during these occasions and have greater opportunity to quarrel. If you think you know someone who is a battered spouse, don't hesitate to call the police. Initial signs of spouse abuse are loud quarreling, screams, or the sound of breaking furniture or dishes.

People have the right to settle their own quarrels. But hopefully you will be able to discern the difference between a private quarrel and a dangerous abusive attack before reporting. Do not hesitate if you suspect someone is in danger. Sometimes men are also victims of spouse abuse. Statistics show that husband beating occurs less frequently than wife beating and is reported less frequently due to the embarrassment involved. The main point to remember is that the victims of abuse will often deny the fact that they are being abused, even defend the abuser's behavior to others. The reasons for this are profound and so varied and many, they are the subject of entire books of their own. It is up to every concerned citizen to report any and all signs of abuse, especially if someone is in danger.

Victims of abuse need help, whether they realize they need it or not. Reporting any suspected abuse is not a violation of anyone's privacy or civil rights. It is your duty as a concerned citizen and fellow human.

VERBAL ABUSE

This type of abuse is not confined to any social class or income. It is due to a lack of love, guidance or discipline in youth. The parent that doesn't bother to ever discipline the child can conceivably do nearly as much damage as the parent who disciplines when unwarranted. Lack of supervision and discipline can occur for a lot of reasons. Often it is unavoidable or unintentional, yet is has an effect on a child's emotions and behavior. Verbal abuse also has several factors to consider. Constant criticism, verbally displayed favoritism towards one child opposed to another, the display of extreme anger in front of a child, blaming a child for a problem or mistake, or actual verbal threats are examples of verbal abuse.

SEXUAL HARRASSMENT

The question of sexual harrasment comes under scrutiny these days. Interested parties, both male and female; judges, lawyers and the media, have voiced their opinions over and over again in print, on the radio, and on television. I do not profess to be an expert or a psychiatrist or any other type of medical expert, however the statements I use in this book are made daily by people in the government, science, business, and medicine. In self-defense it is necessary to view every aspect of a situation in order to broaden an awareness so you may react effectively. In the Bible, John says: "Know your enemies and by so doing you will remain free." Get involved. Learn about local crime activites and the types of crimes committed in your area, so that you have a better chance to remain safe.

SEXUAL ABUSE

Sexual abuse was kept quiet, for many, many years. This has changed recently and today you cannot read the paper or watch television news without hearing of it. As with other forms of abuse, it can be the behavior of a similarly abused parent, but this is not always the case. Often those we trust with the care of our children are responsible, even older children have been known to abuse younger children. If you ever see or suspect such a situation, take immediate steps to remedy the problem. If a child shows signs of being in pain when sitting, walking or performing bodily functions, these could be possible signs of sexual abuse. Other signs are rage or anger, anti-social behavior, preferring isolation to company, problems forming or maintaining friendships, fighting, quarreling, manipulative behavior, and low self-esteem. Often a child's reluctance to go to school, his/her dislike of a teacher, or failure to participate in any activity is due to fear. This fear should be addressed and dealt with, not ignored or glossed over. Often a child abuse victim feels guilty, or afraid to reveal what happened. Sometimes this is because they fear the parent's reaction; other times it is the actual abuser they fear. In either case, if a child shows fear or reluctance to go anywhere without you, and be in the care of other adults or older children, stop and question him/her. The child may not reveal what occurred at first. He or she has been violated in a terrible way, and is perhaps not even old enough to understand what occurred. Slow, patient questioning may get the child to reveal the abuse.

REPORTING CHILD ABUSE

Abusive parents often fail to recognize their own abusive behavior. If they do recognize the problem, they may choose to ignore it, to deny it. Children rarely volunteer to report abuse. They feel alienated, without a friend. Sometimes the abused child is left feeling guilty, as if the abuse was deserved. Similarly wives often cannot bring themselves to report abuse against them. They have been so degraded, so beaten down emotionally and physically they have no strength or self-confidence to pick up the phone and ask for help.

Any type of abuse you strongly suspect should be reported. If you are considering reporting an abuse case there are things to consider:

1. Have you noticed a repeating pattern of abuse or just one incidence?
2. Are your observations unbiased? If so, you can contact your local welfare department to report the case. If you suspect a child is in immediate danger do not hesitate to call the police. When reporting, remember to give your name, if possible.

If for some reason you prefer to remain anonymous that is your option, although the police won't have any witness to the crime to question, which is important. But a child's life is more important so do not hesitate to call police if you fear for any child's safety.

DOMESTIC VIOLENCE CHECKLIST

1. Learn to recognize the signs of child abuse: frequent cuts, bruises, welts or broken bones.
2. Learn to recognize odd behavior in the child: anger, anti-social tendencies, or reluctance to be in another adult's care.
3. Report child abuse to the police and your local welfare agency.
4. Learn to recognize the signs of spouse abuse: screaming, sobbing, or signs of abuse on the body or face.
5. If you are personally being abused, call the police.
6. If you are a victim and wish to make a report, take pictures of your injuries while they're still fresh, make copies of hospital reports or bills, and the names of those to whom you are reporting.
7. If you are a woman being abused by your husband or mate, realize it may happen again. Face the truth, it may never stop as long as you allow it to go on.
8. Don't be a victim! If you are a battered spouse, leave immediately. You can return later with the police to gather your belongings. In extreme situations without family available there are women's shelters for battered spouses.

VIOLENT CRIMES AGAINST WOMEN

RAPE

Rape, by definition, is "carnal knowledge a female forcibly and against her will." Possibly one of the most misunderstood crimes, rape leaves the victim suffering from physical and long-term psychological trauma. Among the physical dangers of rape are: severe beating, internal injury, pregnancy, venereal disease, AIDS, and even death. The emotional toll taken on the rape victim is equally as serious. Rage, humiliation, fear, alienation, and ostracism from the community are among the mental and emotional problems rape victims suffer from.

According to the FBI, a rape is attempted or committed once every five minutes in the United States, with nearly three, fourths of all rapes being committed forcibly against women. Rape is both a violent crime and a sexual assault. Sexual desire is rarely the motivation for rape. It is an act of rage, a desire on the part of the rapist to control, humiliate, and injure a woman. Many states consider all acts of forced sexual contact equal to rape (including rape committed against men by other men or women). Regardless of who the rape victim is, the effects are similar. No one should ever be forced to submit to sexual contact against his/her will. This is violent humiliation taken to the extreme. And the humiliation exists for the victim long after the rape is over, when dealing with the emotional repercussions of the crime.

For some rape victims, denial is a way to deal with the emotional impact of what has occurred. The ordeal of re-living the experience when having to report the rape is often too traumatic for the victim. She may feel that simply not thinking about what happened will make the problem disappear. Perhaps the victim keeps silent because she knows the rapist, and for some reason cannot divulge the rapist's identity. Fear of revenge, concern for children's safety or loss of income can often cause the victim to keep silent. Under no circumstances should you keep silent if you have been sexually assaulted in any way! Please realize that the rapist will do it again (to you or somebody else) if he sees he can get away with it.

Similar to the long term effects of child abuse, rape fosters hostility and mistrust in the victim which affects the way the victim relates to the outside world. If you have been assaulted or raped (or if you know someone who has) report it to the authorities. Keeping silent about any form of sexual abuse is a mistake. Not reporting enables the rapist to rape again. The victim is denying herself/himself, the satisfaction of justice which is their right by law.

PROFILE OF A RAPIST

There is no stereotype of a standard rapist. Rapists come from all ethnic backgrounds and financial brackets. One thing all rapists have in common is that they are severely emotionally disturbed to the point of acting on their aggression. There are many motivations for this. Often the rapist harbors hatred for women because of a poor or violent relationship with his own mother in childhood. Sometimes a problem with the opposite sex causes the rapist to derive sadistic pleasure from humiliating and controlling a woman, hearing her beg for mercy and cry for help.

Statistics show that most rapists are between the ages of 18 and 25. Most rapists are repeat offenders. They may have fairly normal family lives. (It is estimated that over one half of all rapists are married men).

The rapist is basically a stalker, a hunter. The rapist must maintain control so he plans the rape, familiarizing himself with his intended victim's habits and vulnerabilities before striking. Rape falls into three categories:

A. RAPE OF AN ACQUAINTANCE:

Here the rapist knows his intended victim. He may know her personally or he may simply have chosen her and began stalking her. In either case he selects his victim according to vulnerability. He may enjoy resistance when raping, but won't commit the crime unless he is sure he can get away with it.

Statistics show that single working women are the group most frequently targeted by rapists. If you are a single working woman there are ways to protect yourself. Identify the areas of vulnerability in your daily routine. Do you walk through empty parking lots or dark isolated streets at night? If so, you might consider arming yourself with mace, a key defender or a similar personal defense weapon kept close in hand. Enrolling in a martial arts class or a streetwise self-defense course can do much to enhance your personal security. Streetwise self-defense techniques against rape will be covered in a later chapter.

B. RAPE OF FORCED-CONSENT:

Rape of "forced-consent" is defined as: forcing a woman to have sexual relations after the woman has changed her mind from prior consent or suggested consent. Victims of date-rape are often in this category. The common thread in this type of rape is that the rapist refuses to take "NO" for an answer. Whatever the victim did to imply consent, she still has the right to refuse *at any time*, though the rapist fails to realize this. While this type of rape may not be as violent as others, it is no less criminal. It is possible for a dominant or strong-willed person to impose his will on a weaker-willed individual with a minimum of force. Sometimes, too, a man will just force himself on a woman he feels "owes" him sex.

The law determines exactly what constitutes rape, but never forget that you have the right to terminate any sexual contact or implied sexual contact at ANY time. You always have the right to change your mind, in terms of choices. If anyone is imposing his will on you, and you have been trained in defense tactics, you will have an added tool for survival.

C. RAPE ATTACK:

This type of rape is spontaneous. Some rapists are bold enough to victimize total strangers, with no previous plan other than to rape *someone*. This type of rape is always extremely violent. The rapist almost always threatens and controls his victim with deadly force or a weapon. Defense against this type of rape (as well as defense against weapons) will be covered later in this book.

DON'T BE A VICTIM!

A rapist is a criminal. Like all criminals, rapists choose their victims according to vulnerability. Even though rapists may vary in their selection of victims, there are many vulnerable areas common to all victims. Statistics show that the single woman or unescorted woman is the most frequent victim. Friendly or helpful women can also fall victim to rapists. In the mind of the rapist, a friendly person is weak, vulnerable, gullible, and submissive. Often a rapist will make initial contact with a woman by asking for directions, the time or a match etc. Never stop to talk to strangers. If you must, stay alert and confident. Have your mace or defense weapon in hand. It might not be a bad idea to have your weapon in plain sight. Often this is enough to discourage an attacker. The rapist wants to control, but he needs cooperation. If he encounters resistance he is likely to retreat. A woman displaying confident body language is a less likely target than someone who exudes an air of insecurity or fear.

Most rapes occur in the late evening and early morning hours. According to studies, more rapes occur nationwide in the late evening and early morning hours of late summer. If you are a single woman, you are particularly vulnerable. Try to travel among groups of people during these late evening hours.

If you are attacked you have two choices: resist or submit. This is a very personal decision. If you tell the rapist you have AIDS, that your husband is coming, or similar discouragements, it may buy you a few moments, perhaps enough to strike the rapist and escape. However, if you have no option but to submit, try to remember that the rapist is not touching the real you that which is inside. He can only control your body. Try to survive this experience on a mental and emotional level. He cannot take all of you.

If you try to resist, do so immediately! A rapist selects people who appear vulnerable. He does not expect an attack defense. You must strike quickly and effectively to vulnerable areas of his body, and then escape as fast as you can. Many rapes end in death. Your attacker is threatening your life. You must use all deadly force available to you in the first few moments of the attack before you are injured or over-powered. All women should practice streetwise self-defense techniques against rapists.

Strikes to the eyes, nose, ears, throat, solar plexus, groin, and knees can cause great pain when properly delivered, stunning your attacker and making him extremely vulnerable to further strikes. Various combinations of streetwise self-defense techniques will be discussed, enabling you to stop an attacker dead in his tracks and disable him sufficiently to assure your escape.

It is up to you, however, to practice these self-defense techniques to the degree necessary to bring confidence, competence and personal safety.

IF YOU ARE RAPED

If you are raped, seek aid right away. Immediately call the police, then your family if possible. Go directly to a hospital or doctor. Do not change your clothes, or wash yourself, even if injured. You must try to refrain from damaging crucial evidence necessary to convict the rapist. If you go to a hospital, you may wish to also be examined by your own gynecologist; his/her examination may be considerably more complete than one given at a public facility. Get tested for all venereal diseases, especially AIDS, and for pregnancy. Your clothes will also be needed as evidence, so arrange to have a change of clothes if possible. Your doctor or hospital will loan you a garment to wear. Afterwards, bathe, sleep, and begin the process of healing. Healing will take a long time. Allow yourself the time to mourn, get mad, feel bad, sulk, and take care of yourself. For the emotional trauma, seek out competent counseling or a rape crisis center.

Rape crisis centers usually have 24-hour hot lines. Keep their number on your person. You may need it (or want it) when you least expect it. If you do call, you will be connected with a trained counselor and an escort who will be there to advise and accompany you through the medical examinations and criminal justice system. Many rape crisis centers also provide training for medical and legal personnel who interact with the rape victim. Your counselor is trained to be sensitive to your trauma, and will help in many ways. You will receive support and help in regaining and maintaining your dignity and self confidence.

THE EFFECTS OF RAPE

Unlike other crime victims, the rape victim experiences lingering fear, guilt, loss of confidence, embarrassment and anger. The victim may have been beaten and threatened. The rapist often threatens to kill the victim should she report the rape. Once reported, anxiety can linger well after the rapist is captured and imprisoned, if at all.

Guilt hounds many rape victims. Somehow she feels as if she should have or could have resisted more, or tried to escape, even if it was impossible to do so. The victim often feels as if she has lost all control over her life. After being forced to submit to rape, her ability to make decisions is severely hindered. Her will-power diminishes. She is very often too embarrassed to discuss the details of the rape. And therefore the police cannot properly pursue the criminal.

Although still traumatic, anger is a healthier emotion than guilt in terms of emotional survival immediately after the rape. If the anger persists however, the victim may project anger and mistrust of all men, alienating herself from them. Loss of self- esteem and feelings of inferiority are often lingering emotional effects of rape or sexual abuse. When the victim's ability to act or be in control of her life is taken from her, her self-image is severely damaged. It isn't easy to feel like a healthy, happy person after being physically assaulted and treated like an object. The intention of the rapist is to humiliate his victim. Hopefully the victim will eventually heal enough to realize her ordeal was over after the rape. It is the rapist who has the problem, and who will always have to deal with it. By giving in to feelings of inferiority, fear, guilt, embarrassment, and lack of control, the victim is allowing the rapist the satisfaction of having succeeded in his attempt. It is the reaction to the rape which the rapist seeks, that of terror and humiliation. The act of rape is only the vehicle the rapist uses to accomplish this.

If you have been raped, there is still more you can do to not be a victim. You are a victim only when you feel victimized. Once you are safe you will still feel the lingering effects of victimization. Many rape victims help in rape crisis centers or similar groups as a means of helping themselves and other rape victims. Often by helping others who have similarly suffered, the recovering victim can more quickly recover as well.

There is little in the way of compensation for rape victims. Although many states do have laws allowing victims some form of compensation, many victims feel as if no sum of money will suffice. Seeing the rapist caught, convicted, and sentenced is probably the best compensation. Reporting any sexual abuse or rape and cooperating with law enforcement officials in their investigation is one step towards preventing future rapes.

All women should practice streetwise self-defense precautions to guard against rape. Prevention is the key.

RAPE PREVENTION CHECKLIST

1. Practice streetwise precautions mentioned previously in this book.
2. Practice the streetwise self-defense techniques discussed in the next chapter of this book until you are competent at them.
3. Involve all family members in precautionary measures, including self-defense.
4. Urge your daughter to travel in groups.
5. Discuss the possibility of date rape with your daughter.
6. Always keep track of your children's location and let someone know your itinerary.
7. Always carry mace, a key defender, or similar weapon on your person.
8. If attacked, and unable to escape, try an emotional appeal like crying. This may lessen the severity of the attack. The rapist thinks of the victim as an object. If you can get him talking, you may even thwart the attack.
9. If conversing with the rapist, try to subtly placate his ego. In some case it is possible to give him the emotional gratification he seeks this way.
10. To resist an attack, you must try to deliver an attack defense *immediately* before you are injured, and while the rapist still expects no resistance. Attack vulnerable areas with deadly force, using the techniques discussed in this book.
11. Learn enough about self-defense to deal with any possible scenario. What if you are surprised by an attacker wielding a gun? If you want to try resistance under any circumstances practice the techniques in this book, and consider a martial arts class or a streetwise self-defense class.
12. If you have been raped, immediately report it to police.
13. Call your family and/or rape crisis center.
14. Do not bathe or change your clothes. Bring a change of clothes to the doctor's or to the hospital.
15. If you can, write down all details of the incident while it is still fresh in your mind, or record them on tape.
16. Don't be afraid to talk about the rape, and seek help if you can. The rape crisis centers are staffed by people trained to help.
17. Get checked out by your regular gynecologist.

Streetwise Self-defense and the Law

All people have the right to defend themselves when faced with a threatening situation, especially when threatened with physical violence. Understanding what legally constitutes "reasonable and necessary force" is important, especially once you've begun your practice of self-defense techniques. Martial arts and other self-defense training offer techniques designed to teach you to defend yourself, and can be deadly once mastered. Black Belt martial artists can use deadly force in self-defense against an aggressor, terminating in death or severe injury for the aggressor rather than the victim, thanks to self-defense techniques.

In any self-defense case resulting in injury or death there will be an investigation, perhaps a hearing, possibly resulting in the prosecution of the individual who used deadly force as a self-defense technique. It is the responsibility of anyone learning self-defense techniques designed to injure an opponent to investigate what the laws are regarding self-defense. If you do not wish to face prosecution, or if you need to prove "justifiable force," you need to better acquaint yourself with the law. All criminal charges are based on the premise of "legal public wrong doing;" that which affects the public or society at large. If convicted of a criminal charge you could be fined, imprisoned, or both! Legal wrong doing can be considered either civil or criminal in the eyes of the law. If you are found liable in a civil case you may be ordered as the defendant to pay compensatory and punitive damages to the victim even if he was going to attack you and make *you* the victim. Remember that a single act can possibly result in two prosecutions: civil and criminal. Your circumstances and injuries you suffered are considered by judge and/or by jury to determine whether "sufficient cause" existed to warrant the use of a "forcible defense."

REASONABLE FORCE

Excessive or extreme force exists in many self-defense cases, with anger motivating you to defend yourself, and potentially creating a legal problem for yourself. What you want to learn is "reasonable force." Reasonable self-defense could be defined as: the use of only enough force to achieve the desired result and *no more*. What is reasonable and necessary is not considered extreme or excessive by the law, although what constitutes reasonable force varies from state to state. Contact your county prosecutor's office to familiarize yourself with the laws regarding reasonable force and self-defense in your state. In most cases laws throughout the country agree that "reasonable and necessary force" is: that which is needed to resist immediate danger that could result in injury or death. The aggressor must threaten you with injury or death before you can defend yourself. And you will be required to prove this should you need to use a plea of self-defense in court.

DEFENDING A FRIEND OR FAMILY MEMBER

If you find yourself in a situation where you are considering coming to someone's aid, please realize that by interfering with an act of violence you might place the intended victim in even greater danger. There is no law that requires you to come to anyone's aid regardless of his/her personal peril. But it you feel the situation warrants it, keep in mind you will be legally required to prove it in a court of law.

Legally, you are only justified if the individual being attacked clearly cannot defend him or herself against injury. Both you and the victim will be required to prove the truth of the nature of the attack. Should the victim be injured at all during the attack, you could find yourself faced with a lawsuit against you for interfering. The victim could claim that, until you interfered the situation was under control. In such cases, proving that your interference did not endanger the victim is nearly impossible. To a judge or jury it could seem quite feasible that your actions actually escalated the situation resulting in the injury or death of the victim. If the victim is killed in such an encounter you might be sued by the victim's family. Enraged and seeking revenge, the victim's family could fasten their blame on you for the loss of a loved one.

With this in mind it becomes clear that anyone practicing self-defense should have a basic knowledge of his or her state's laws regarding self-defense and the use of violent force in any situation. Hopefully, if you adhere to legal, moral, and social standards, you can expect a fair verdict if prosecuted.

DEFENDING YOUR PROPERTY

Generally speaking, if your property is violated, or being illegally threatened, the use or threat of force may be necessary if law enforcement is not present at the time. In this situation you are not on the street or in public. You are home and trouble comes to you in the form of a criminal threat, either to your person, property, or both.

If someone has entered your property or home to commit a crime, and you have verbally warned the criminal about possible use of force and/or weapons against him, you are then justified to use whatever force is necessary. Granted, all situations have variables, such as the speed of the attack, time of day and visibility. Remember that, in any violent attack or violent defense, there are laws to which we are all accountable determining justifiable and necessary force.

WHAT YOU SHOULD KNOW ABOUT WEAPONS

Firearms have become prolific in America today. Many people believe guns should be illegal and only issued to law enforcement officers and the military. But many other people believe guns, used properly, are a useful form of self-defense. As a martial artist, I feel in a crime situation a gun can be taken from the owner and in turn used on them. The martial artist practices many hours per week to attain a level of proficiency which would calculate the chance of removing a gun from the threatening hands of a criminal. Even then, the martial artists realizes the dangerous conditions and the possibility of losing his/her life. It is best to give the criminal whatever he or she wants. Additionally, the defender may be successful, and wound or kill his attacker. In such a case, the defender may be arrested and charged with assault or murder.

Understanding what constitutes safe, effective and legal, weaponry is to your advantage and necessary if you own a weapon. The laws governing the sale and use of weapons as a means of self-defense are again based on the concept of reasonable force, within the framework of society's moral and ethical codes. According to the second amendment, each citizen of the U.S. has the right to own firearms (except minors and felons). Of course the purchase or use of weapons is strictly regulated regarding where and when the weapon may be carried or discharged, and who may own a weapon.

Although it is a matter of individual choice, many feel the presence of a weapon in a home where children are present constitutes an additional threat rather than a security measure, and accidental death statistics in such cases have proved this is sometimes true. For the individual home owner fully acquainted with the use of firearms, owning a weapon may be as common place as any other hardware in the home. In either case, if safety is practiced the chances of an accident are reduced. It is up to the home owner to decide what degree of potential danger a weapon represents. In a home where firearms are kept, there should be established rules for safe-guarding family members. Just as you would not allow your young child access to your car, you must take a similar attitude regarding firearms. Not only must weapons be locked up, all family members need to know the danger of using them without adult supervision. Explain to children that firearms can kill, but only when a person uses them. Remind your family that one single oversight or neglect in following safety precautions could result in death.

If you are considering purchasing a weapon, there are a few facts to consider. Realize that there are a wide range of weapons available to suit every need. Take the time to fully investigate and test what is available. Realize that this is just as important a decision as your original decision to purchase a weapon.

A weapon is designed to protect you in a life-threatening situation. It is not meant for aggression. Many objects can be used as a weapon rather than firearms. A knife, frying pan, pen, pencil, or even your car keys can be used to defend yourself. Hair spray or almost any aerosol can blind an attacker temporarily. An umbrella or cane can be used in public places. If you examine your surroundings you will realize your home contains many self-defense weapons.

USING A CLUB OR KNIFE

A club can be an extremely forceful instrument with which to strike and defend yourself. Placing police batons, short sticks, baseball bats, hockey sticks, or golf clubs strategically in your home can prepare you for useful defense against an attacker. If you find you must use such a weapon you must remember to have a firm grip on the handle. Remember an attacker will use the weapon on you if he can take it from you. Use the weapon only to disable your attacker. Never continue to strike your attacker once he is disabled or you may find yourself facing an assault charge. Again, the key here is "reasonable force."

If attacked with a weapon, first try striking his arms or hands, followed by a strike to the legs to overpower him. If you can, avoid striking

the head, as this can be fatal in some cases.

The knife is the world-wide weapon of choice. Both a weapon and a tool, knives are found in every household. You do not have to be a seasoned knife fighter to handle a knife effectively. The basic concepts involving knife defense, if studied properly, can teach you effective defensive and offensive techniques should you need them. Knives are available in a variety of sizes and designs. A hunter's knife is designed to be used outdoors, for skinning game, fileting a fish, etc. A commando's knife has a double edge razor sharp blade so it cannot be easily grabbed from your hand, also providing a clean, double-cut slice. The common kitchen knife isn't always razor sharp, and may have a rounded edge, but if used effectively and with power behind it in an attack against a vital area the kitchen knife can prove to be quite effective.

WEAPONS CHECKLIST

1. Obtain all weapons over the counter from a legally licensed dealer.
2. When in serious doubt about a weapons dealer, report him to authorities.
3. Learn and practice weapons safety precautions.
4. Keep weapons locked away at all times.
5. Equip firearms with a trigger guard, to keep them from being discharged accidently.
6. Be sure your purchased weapon is equipped with a serial number on it somewhere.
7. Obtain a bill of sale for your weapon, and register it with local police.
8. Never play games with a weapon, such as pointing a firearm at someone even if it's empty.
9. Keep all weapon ammunition properly locked in a safe location.
10. Always assume a firearm is loaded and double check whenever handling it.
11. Never handle weapons when using alcohol.
12. Clean and oil your firearm regularly.
13. Never discharge old ammunition.
14. Always empty and dry-fire (pull the trigger) your firearm before storing.
15. Practice emergency procedures for use of any weapon in case of need. Remember this is not a game, and make sure all family members understand this.

Streetwise Self-defense

BASIC TECHNIQUES

Before you can defend yourself adequately, you must learn and practice certain basic techniques-the building blocks of self-defense. As you master these basic techniques and acquire new knowledge and skills, your awareness of mental and physical powers will also grow, and you will develop the total coordination and muscle control you need to defend yourself with confidence.

If you are serious about learning to defend yourself, you will put as much effort and concentration into it as you can. I strongly recommend that you devote at least one hour a day to the practice of the basic stances, blocks, strikes, and falls. If you get involved in self-defense heavily enough, you will find within your mind and body the inner strength that can come only from dedicated practice. This inner force has been called *Ki* by the Japanese. The essence of this difficult concept lies in the idea that the strength of a person cannot be determined by physical strength alone. Both mind and body must be unified before true power can be achieved. From time to time we hear of people who perform amazing feats of strength in moments of great stress; for example, someone lifts a car to free someone who is trapped. The only reason the first person could lift the car was that his or her mind and body, which normally function separately, were instinctively unified. For the self-defense woman, *Ki* is a goal to strive for the ability to unify her mind and body at will and fully tap her potential strength and energy.

Always warm up and stretch at the beginning of your practice session. Don't tire yourself out; just do enough to get relaxed and loose. Practice the basic stances during your warm-up, in addition to traditional exercises, such as sit-ups, push-ups, leg stretches, and jumping jacks. Play special attention so that your feet are placed in a slightly pigeon-toed position, gripping the floor. Tense your body and expel all the air from your lungs. Then slowly breathe in again and relax. Assume the other stances and practice moving from one to another. These should become familiar to you, and you should feel natural in them, ready to move in attack or defense. Throughout your practice session, try to begin and end each movement from one of these stances so that you develop the habit of always being in a balanced position ready for a new movement in any direction. Go slowly and concentrate on accuracy; speed will follow.

Before we move on to the basic blocks, strikes, and falls, let us look for a moment at the importance of *Kiai* to your self-defense. In practical terms, *Kiai* is a loud shout that you should incorporate into all your practice exercises. If you are grabbed by an attacker, a loud, self-asserting yell will very probably instill your assailant with fright or shock. At least it should throw him momentarily off balance. *Kiai* is more, however, than a mere shock tactic. Kiai is both psychologically and physiologically effective. The expulsion of air through your lungs increases your strength. It is not enough just to yell; you must expel all the air from your throat and diaphragm. You should be able to feel all your muscles tighten at the moment of expulsion. Properly done, a Kiai will help you attain maximum strength while at the same time frightening your attacker.

Practice Kiai with all the basic movements: strikes, blocks, and falls. Do not be embarrassed; it may someday save your life.

You can begin your practice for self-defense alone, using a mirror, until you feel comfortable in your movements. Use the horse rider's stance as the starting point for blocks and hand strikes. (For kicks you will use the other three basic stances: the forward stance, cat stance, and side stance). As you progress and gain confidence, find someone to be your partner. You can take turns assuming the attacker's role and practicing the basic defenses described in this book.

Let us take a look at the positions of the hand that you will use for most of the strikes and grabs in your self-defense arsenal. The hands are two of the most important weapons you have. There are many different hand positions and strikes beyond the traditional fist punch. With the hand held flat, you can use the fingertips to thrust or you can chop with either edge of the hand ("the "knife-edge" or the "inside knife-edge"). The illustrations show the portions of the hand used to deliver the blow. With the hand in a fist position, you can strike with the knuckles straight on or with the backfist; you can strike down or across with the hammerfist and reverse hammerfist. You can open your fist part way and strike with the heel of your hand. A variation of this strike is the "palm hand" strike, in which your hand is cupped. Finally, by opening the cup into a claw, you are ready for a "claw hand strike," usually aimed at the eyes or the Adam's apple. As you practice these strikes in the mirror, go slowly and concentrate on form and balance; speed and self-confidence will follow.

When you begin to practice with a partner, you should spend a part of each session working on your grabs. Grabs are used when your attacker's hand has come to rest somewhere on your person. You can grab your attacker's hand from either side with one or both hands; the object is to put painful pressure on his wrist. With an outside wristlock, you turn the attacker's hand so that his thumb rotates up, over, and away from his body at the same time his wrist bends toward his forearm. Press with your thumb or thumbs as hard as you can into the back of his hand. With an inside wristlock, you turn the attacker's hand down, under, and back, at the same time you put pressure on the wrist as before. The third basic grab is the downward wristlock. Grab the attacker's hand with both of yours and force his wrist back and down.

Kicks may be delivered with the ball or heel of your foot, with either side of your foot, or with the instep. You may kick up or sideways, or you may punch with your foot. You can use the side of a shoe or its heel to rake or scrape an attacker if he has you from behind, and of course you can stamp down on his instep.

In addition to the offensive movements, you should incorporate defensive movements into each practice session. In the following pages you will see a dozen blocks and falls illustrated. You can practice these movements alone, but you should use a partner as soon as possible. Again, begin slowly and concentrate on balance and form. When you practice blocks, get used to using them when moving forward and when falling back. If you are attacked, you must always move forward if you see the strike coming in time and backward when the strike is already moving quickly toward you. You should move immediately from a block into a strike or a fall.

As you acquire self-confidence and ability, you should build into your practice sessions the goal of a continuous series of movements. If you are attacked, you will not make a move and wait to see what happens; you must carry out a constant counterattack until you are out of danger. The strikes you will be practicing are done while the attacker has you in a bear hug one from behind, one from the front. Practice each series first to the left side and then to the right. Do all the strikes in succession, slowly at first, then with moderate speed, and finally with full speed. You should begin, as you gain confidence, to develop a definite sense of where and how to strike and how much force to use.

STRIKES AGAINST VULNERABLE AREAS

In this chapter, we will deal with the natural weapons of your body-your hands, feet, elbows, and knees-and with the vulnerable target areas of your attacker's body. Neither the size of these natural weapons nor your own physical strength is the major factor in immobilizing an attacker. It is, rather, the precise timing and delivery of a strike to a vital area. What about the amount of force needed to stop an attacker? If you are attacked, you must strike as hard and as fast as you can, for the attacker is out to hurt you. But remember that it is your form and speed which are the major sources of the force you have available. With practice, you will soon realize that you have sufficient force to defend yourself and to immobilize an attacker if you have to. The techniques you are acquiring are designed specifically to maximize the force delivered by a strike. The target areas you will become familiar with are all highly vulnerable. In the illustrations which follow, you will see which blows are likely to be most effective against the various vulnerable target areas on your attacker, from his eyes to his feet. First, however, let us review what damage you can do with a well-aimed hand, foot, elbow, or knee.

You can counterattack easily at many areas above your attacker's shoulders. His eyes, ears, nose, temples, forehead, and neck all are very vulnerable. Any blow to these areas will cause great pain and may well disable an attacker. A strike to the eyes can easily cause temporary or permanent blindness. A blow to the nose can knock a man out; or at least it will cause his eyes to water uncontrollably. A cupped hand strike to the ears can rupture the eardrum or fracture the jaw; it could knock a man out. If you miss the ears and hit the jaw hinge or the temples, or if you aim for the temples, the blow can still be effective. A blow to the forehead can fracture the skull or the frontal sinus and cause either a slight or a major concussion. Aim for the front or side of the throat and you can damage any of the organs located there. If you strike your attacker at the back of the neck, you can cause whiplash or a broken neck. A hard hit on the top of a vertebra or spinal disc can cause paralysis anywhere below the blow. Do not worry about what you may do to the attacker; remember what he is trying to do to you, and remember that he will do it if you don't stop him first!

The trunk of the body provides larger and more readily available targets. Just a moderate blow to the rib cage can break some ribs. If ribs are broken, at the very least your attacker will have trouble breathing and you will gain time to continue your counterattack or to escape. A hard blow to the collarbone can fracture it, paralyzing part of all of the arm on that side. Below the rib cage, you can attack the diaphragm, solar plexus, kidneys, spleen, bladder, and groin. Striking in the diaphragm (the solar plexus region, just below the frontal rib cage) can knock the wind out of an attacker, leaving him at your mercy. It might knock him out or rupture an internal organ, such as his stomach, gall bladder, or pancreas. It might even collapse a lung. Any such injury could send your attacker into shock. Blows to the kidneys, to the spleen on the left side of the abdomen, to the bladder, and to the groin might cause internal bleeding, leading to nausea, pain, and/or dizziness.

Your attacker's limbs are vulnerable also. A broken elbow or knee cap is extremely painful and immobilizing. A hard blow on the shin or foot can splinter the bone and temporarily stop your attacker. Any of the wristlocks shown in chapter 1 can be used to break the wrist or to cause extreme pain. Remember that after any blow to a limb, even an effective one, you will have to follow up with another strike and possibly another.

Study and learn the strikes and targets in this chapter and put them together into patterns of continuous movement. Each blow is not just a blow in self-defense, it is, a step toward the next blow. You must be prepared to fight until you are out of danger.

USING YOUR PERSONAL ITEMS AS WEAPONS

No one is allowed to carry a concealed weapon. It is not against the law, however, to carry personal articles such as keys, a hair brush, a comb or a pen. Nor is it illegal to carry a cane or an umbrella. Any of these articles make effective weapons, and you should work them into your practice routine.

Counter attacks using pocketbook items, canes and umbrellas in the following pictures of this section. Remember that you must have such weapons within easy reach if they are to be of any use to you. Don't bury your keys in your pocketbook! Carry them in your pocket and put other pocketbook items in your other pocket.

You could also use a tool known as a "Uwara Stick." It is the length of a pencil and the width of a broom handle. It serves as a very effective streetwise self-defense tool, and it is very easy to carry.

ATTACK AND COUNTER-ATTACK

Rape can occur anywhere at any time. A rapist does not care where or when he attacks. In an environment in which there are many people about, he may approach you nonviolently at first and then threaten you if you do not respond favorably. Perhaps he will pinch your neck or twist your arm. The majority of rapes, however, take place in secluded areas, where no help is handy. They are violent, aggressive, brutal, and sometimes fatal.

If you are to defend yourself, you must learn, first of all, to overcome fear and panic. You must be ready to act quickly with a succession of blocks, strikes, and evasions. The more you practice the basic techniques and strikes presented in the first two chapters, the more confident you will become in your own power and in your ability to defend yourself. You will be ready to counter-attack spontaneously. Balance, speed, and control will be built into your reactions.

In the following pages, a number of possible attacks are pictured, as well as suggested defenses. Use these as the bases for your practice exercises, and remember that you should be able to move either left or right. Practice each defense to both sides. When you feel confident in the moves pictured here, invent variations of your own and responses to other conceivable attacks.

If you are faced with more than one attacker, use your judgement. If you can disable one attacker quickly, you stand a good chance of scaring off the rest. Survey the area for any possible weapons such as sticks or stones. When you counter-attack the first assailant, try to use his body as a shield; use an armlock or a grab to the carotid artery. One final reminder: do not forget your shout! It increases the force of your strike and it will confuse your attacker.

HOW TO PREVENT INJURIES

In the martial arts (as in any sport), you are naturally in a situation where you might get injured. Most injuries can be prevented by using protective equipment, keeping alert to your opponent, and by studying the proper techniques. While practicing the martial arts, never catch your partner by surprise or fool around when you should be serious.

As you begin your training there is a possibility of muscle soreness or injury. Stretching exercises are necessary to limber up the body. Whenever you do a new exercise or movement, you use muscles that are not accustomed to the activity. As a result, they will become sore. Do not let this discourage you from working out. As you repeat the same exercises and movements your muscles begin to strengthen and develop.

The best indication of limbered-up muscles is a feeling of warmth throughout your body. This means you are ready to go.

Occasionally, it is difficult to detect an injury since it may not hurt right away. However, if you do feel any pain, have a hard time moving one of your muscles or joints, or if you see some swelling or a bruise, be sure to rest and notify your doctor. Never work out when you feel pain; you will only make your injury worse.

These basic rules should be followed when you work out:

1.Take your time. Don't rush your exercises. Warming up is essential for all athletes.

2.Always concentrate on what you are doing. Don't let your mind wander.

3.If you are tired, don't force yourself to work out. Most injuries occur when you don't have the energy to exercise properly, and your body needs rest.

4.Never over-train. Only work out to your limit. Forcing yourself will just make you weak.

5.Never eat a large meal immediately before or after you work out. Always wait at least a half-hour, so that your body will be able to digest the food properly.

A WORD ABOUT NUTRITION

Although exercise and self-defense training are important methods for maintaining physical fitness,they cannot be performed without adhering to a proper diet.

When the word diet is used, it does not only refer to a low-caloric intake. As you exercise and burn up calories, as well as needed nutrients, you have to replace them by eating three well-balanced meals per day.

Food is fuel for the body. Without it, your body cannot perform and develop properly. If your body lacks proteins or other nutrients and minerals, you will not achieve the muscle development or tone that is the goal of exercise. You will fatigue easily and become susceptible to excessive soreness. Avoid junk foods (empty calories) and eat foods that are rich in the nutrients and minerals your body needs (non-fatty meats, chicken, fish, vegetables, milk, cheese, eggs, whole-wheat breads, and cereals, nuts, fruits, and raisins for snacks). Remember, do not go overboard on any one food. Follow a varied diet.

In your martial arts streetwise self defense training, you will demand a lot from your body. Feed it well!

STANCES

1—TENSION STANCE

This stance is most commonly used when you are doing a tension exercise. Your feet are slightly pigeon—toed, bent, and gripping the floor.

2—SIDE STANCE

Place one of your feet on the side of the knee of the other leg, as you face toward the side of the bent leg. You are now ready to snap out a side kick to any part of your attacker's body.

3—FORWARD STANCE

Place your feet about shoulder—width apart, at a forty—five degree angle to each other. Bend your forward leg, while keeping your back leg straight.

HORSE RIDER'S STANCE

With your upper body crouched over, bend your knees and feet slightly. You should feel as though your legs are straddled across the back of a horse; hence this stance is called the horse rider's stance.

CAT STANCE

With one leg bent and facing toward your side, bend your other leg in front of you. The heel of your forward foot should be up and facing the side of your rear foot. The forward foot is now in a position to kick.

STRIKES

FINGERTIP THRUST

RIDGE HAND

KNUCKLE FIST

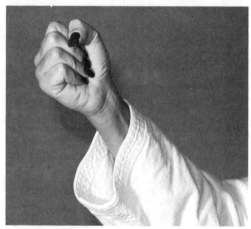

HAMMERFIST

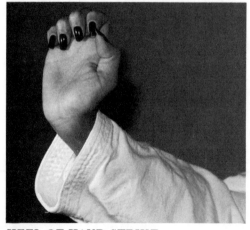

HEEL OF HAND STRIKE

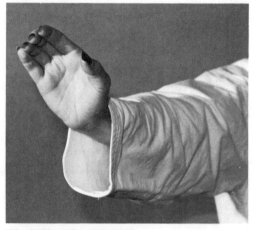

CLAWHAND STRIKE

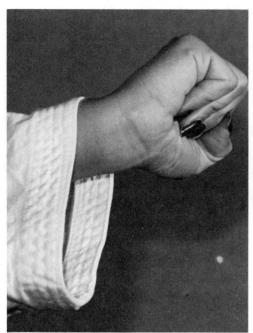

REVERSE HAMMERFIST

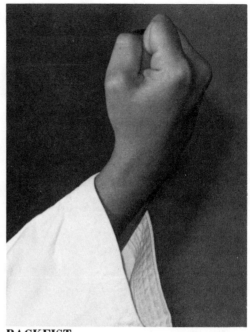

BACKFIST

PALMHAND STRIKE

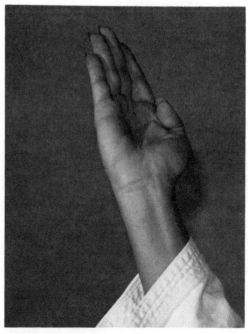

KNIFE-EDGE STRIKE

GRABS

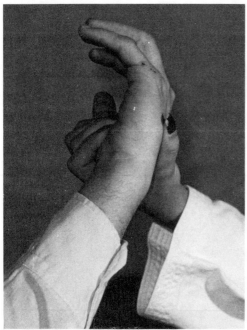

ONE HAND OUTSIDE WRIST LOCK

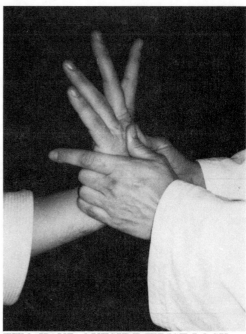

TWO-HAND OUTSIDE WRIST LOCK

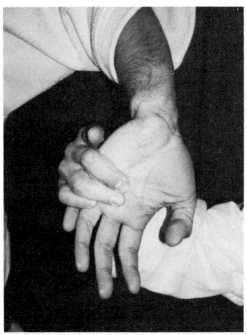

ONE-HAND INSIDE WRIST LOCK

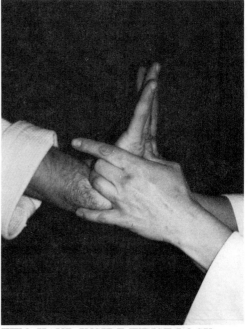

TWO-HAND INSIDE WRIST LOCK
DOWNWARD WRIST LOCK

BLOCKS

HIGH BLOCK

In a counterclockwise motion, swing around and block a facial strike with your forearm. Your arm should always be bent at the elbow.

HIGH BLOCK WITH FIST

Same technique as the High Bock, but as you are blocking, the palm of your hand is in a fist position, palm turned so that it is facing your attacker, and closed tightly.

BLOCKS

INSIDE MIDDLE BLOCK

With your elbow staying down near your mid-section, your forearm comes around in front of you in a counterclockwise motion. Keeping your fist clenched tightly, your forearm will block your attacker's strike directly to the outside.

OUTSIDE MIDDLE BLOCK

As you step to the outside with your foot, or move into a cat stance position, your forearm comes out in front of you with your elbow bent. Now swing across the front of your body with the forearm and block your attacker's midsection strike.

SWEEPING LOWER BLOCK

As your attacker is punching to your groin or kicking you, come up across your body, with your elbow bent. Now drive it downward and swing across your body to block your attacker's strike.

CHICKENHEAD BLOCK WITH BACK OF WRIST

As your attacker punches to your face, squat down low and drive the back of your wrist directly up the middle of your body. Now guide your attacker's face punch directly upward past your face.

FALLS—BACK BREAKFALL

1 With your feet apart, squat slightly downward with your hands in front of you.

2 Now kick out your feet and proceed to fall backward.

3 As you fall, keep your head up and look between your legs. Keep your arms straight out at your sides so that when you hit the ground they can absorb the shock of your body weight.

FALLS—FORWARD BREAKFALL

1 Step forward with your right foot, preparing to put your right hand on the ground.

2 Now kick your left leg up toward the ceiling and push off your right foot. Tuck your head down.

3 In completing the roll, keep your legs apart so that your knees don't hit each other. You are on your left side with left hand at your side, right hand on your stomach, so there will be no damage to your back.

FALLS—SIDE BREAKFALL

1 Kick your right foot out toward the left front.

2 Proceed to fall to your right side.

3 As you fall to your right side, your right arm hits the ground next to you, with your left hand on your stomach.

FORWARD FACE FALL

1 Place your hands in front of you, your feet about shoulder-width apart.

2 Now kick your feet out from underneath you, with your hands in front, so they are ready for the point of impact.

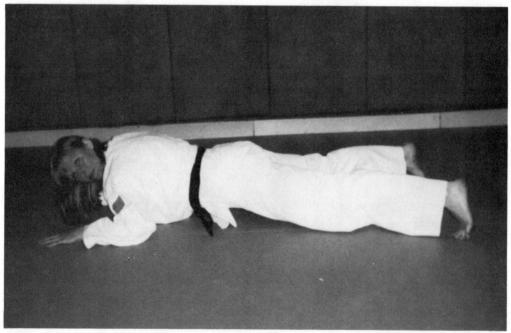

3 Turn your head to the left side as your forearms and hands strike the mat. Your body should be suspended in the air with the balls of your feet and your forearms holding you up. Your elbows do not hit the mat.

1 Your attacker has you pined against your car with your arms up.

2 You are now striking with your knee straight up into your attacker's groin.

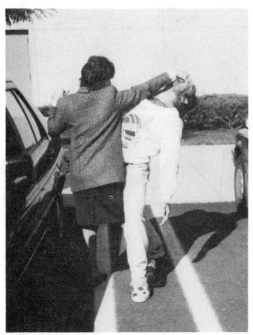

3 You are now striking your attacker's eyes as you hook his leg and drive him backward.

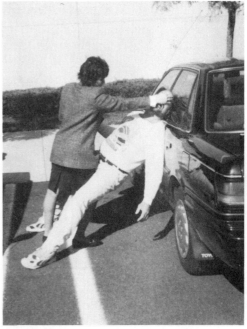

4 You complete the move by driving your attacker backward as your leg attacks his groin and your hand attacks his eyes.

1 Your attacker is pulling you out of your car as you are about to get in.

2 With your left hand in a hammer fist position, you immediately strike downward to your attacker's groin.

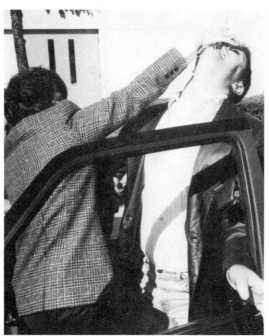

3 With your keys in your right hand immediately turn and attack your attacker's face with your knee striking his groin.

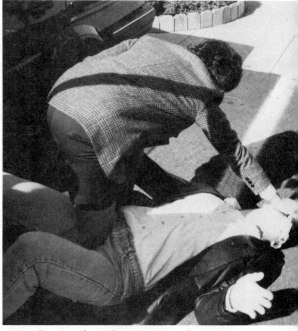

4 To complete the move you drive your attacker straight to the ground with your knee to groin and hand full of keys to his face.

1 As you attempt to get in your car your attacker grabs you with his hand covering your mouth. You immediately strike you attacker's hand with your keys.

3 You now proceed to strike your attacker's groin while maintaining control of his opposite arm.

4 As you maintain control of the arm you start to rotate to the rear maintaining control of his elbow and hand.

4 You are now driving your attacker straight back in an arm bar lock.

5 As you drive your attacker back simultaneously lock his arm up and strike to his groin with your knee this will complete the move.

1 Unexpectedly your attacker grabs you from behind as he proceeds to slide his right hand into your blouse.

2 You immediately grab his fingers turning them in an upward motion causing severe pain.

3 You now bring your attackers hand straight down locking his fingers up as his elbow is locked across your shoulder simultaneously you elbow strike him to his groin.

4 You then proceed to bring his arm over your head and down as you lock his elbow and fingers.

5 Complete the move by bringing your attacker straight to the ground breaking his fingers and applying pressure to his throat.

1 Your attacker is sitting next to you attempting to physically harass you.

2 He now has his arm around your shoulder as you attempt to keep him away.

3 You now proceed to wrap your arm directly around your attacker's arm as you strike with a ride hand to your attacker's throat.

4 You complete the movement by driving your attacker down with an armbar lock and a choke hold.

1 Your attacker is about to choke you from a frontal position.

2 As you grab your attacker's wrist to maintain control you strike with a ridge hand to his groin.

3 You now stand up holding your attacker's wrist as you strike to the eyes with your opposite hand.

4 As you turn your attacker in a downward wrist locking position you lay him over the bench you elbow strike to his lower area. You complete the move by striking to the throat or eye area.

1 Your attacker is attempting to assault you at your desk with a grab and a strike.

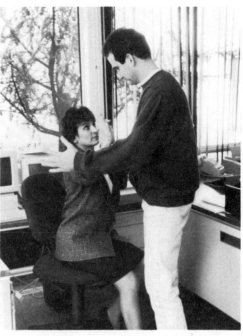

2 You are now blocking with your right hand as your attacker attempts to attack you.

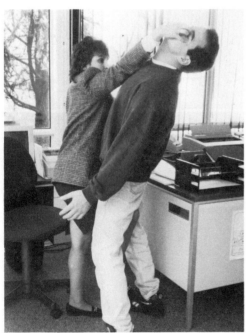

3 As your right knee comes up to your attacker's groin you are striking with your fingers to your attacker's eyes.

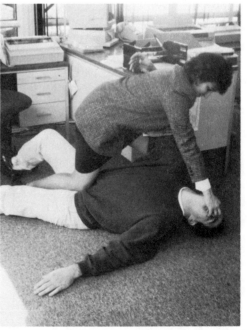

4 You complete the movement by driving your attacker to the ground with your knee in his groin and fingers in his eyes.

1 Your attacker is attempting to assault you from the rear as you are sitting at your desk.

2 While grabbing your attacker's left hand with your right you proceed to slide your chair back and strike with your elbow to his groin.

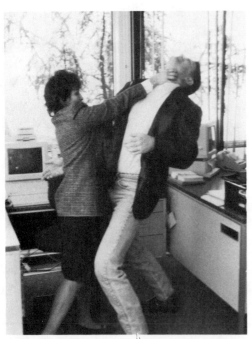

3 You immediately strike to your attacker's throat with your right hand as you proceed to get up out of your chair.

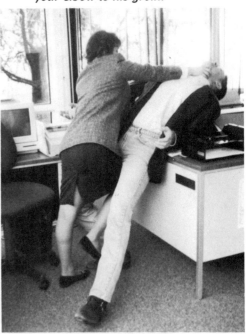

4 You drive your attacker across the desk as your right knee strikes his groin and your right hand continues to strike his throat.

1 *Your attacker makes a physical attempt from the front.*

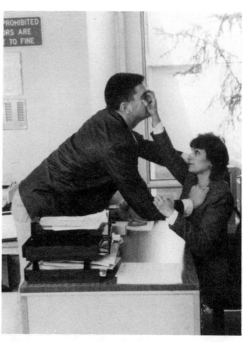

2 *You immediately grab his arm with your left hand and proceed to strike with a blinding finger attack to the attacher's eye using your right hand.*

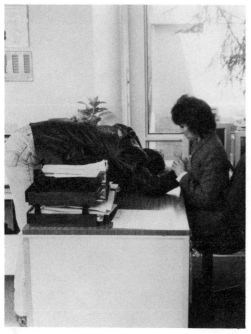

3 *Grabbing your attacker's wrist in a downward motion you lay him across the desk face down.*

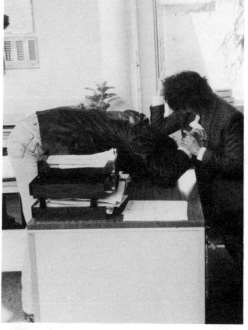

4 *Completing the move by striking with your elbow to the base of your attacker's neck.*

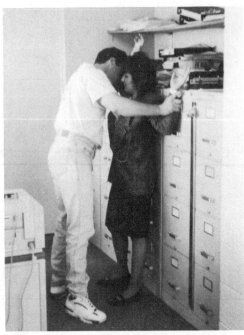

1 Your attacker is about to physically assault you against the file cabinets.

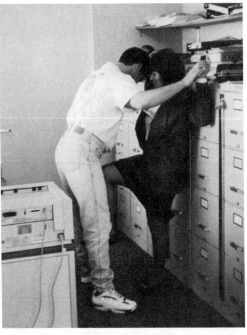

2 Your first defensive action is to strike with your knee to your attacker's groin bringing him forward.

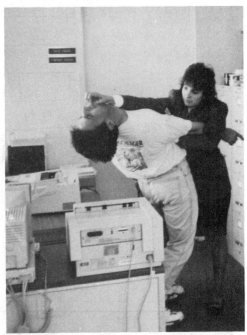

3 Due to the force of impact to your attacker groin he will immediately let go, you then lock up his right arm as you attack with an open hand strike to his chin or nose.

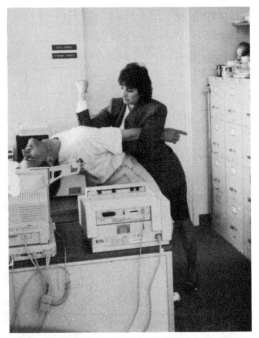

4 You complete the move by driving your attacker across the desk with an arm bar break and elbow strike to his clavicle.

Striking the eyes with fingertips. This strike is usually made with your feet far apart and one leg slightly in front of the other. Grab a body part, such as the arm, if you can, and pull your attacker forward as you strike.

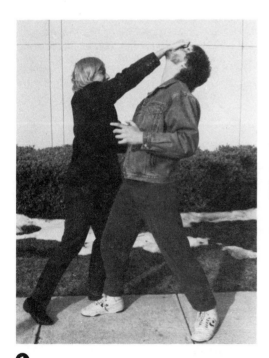 

❶ ❷

Striking under the nose with (1) palm-hand or (2) knife-edge. With your feet shoulder-width apart and your right leg slightly in front of you, move toward your attacker and strike into his nose, driving him backward.

Striking the front or side of the throat with (1) claw-hand, (2) knife-edge, or (3) inside knife-edge. Put your right leg forward and strike your attacker in his throat. If you can grab your attacker, pull him toward you at the same time.

1   **2**

Striking the back of the neck with (1) hammer-first or (2) downward elbow strike. If your attacker is bent over, strike down, at the same time squatting down with him. If you need to, you can also drive his face into your knee.

1   **2**

Striking the temple with (1) elbow or (2) backfist. In these movements, a wrist-lock is applied with the elbow. Step forward and drive your other elbow into your attacker's temple or strike it with a backfist. Your feet should be apart in a balanced stance at the end of either strike.

❶
Striking the bridge of the nose with forehand. Step in with your right foot and pull your attacker's wrist toward you as you strike.

❶

Striking the ears with cupped hands. This strike is useful when your attacker has you immobile, but your hands are free. Strike the tops of his ears with the palms of both hands as hard as you can.

▶ VULNERABLE AREAS

Striking the jawbone with (1) elbow, (2) palm-hand, or (3) knee. Strike upward as you step forward and pull your attacker toward you by the wrist.

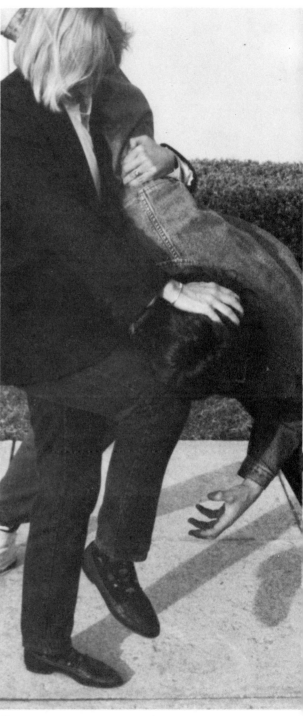

❶ **❷**

Striking the center of the forehead with (1) or (2) knee. As you strike with your elbow, try to grab your attacker's head with your opposite hand and pull his head into the blow. As you drive your knee up into your attacker's head push down on the back of his head with your hand. This can be done from the armbar lock, as illustrated.

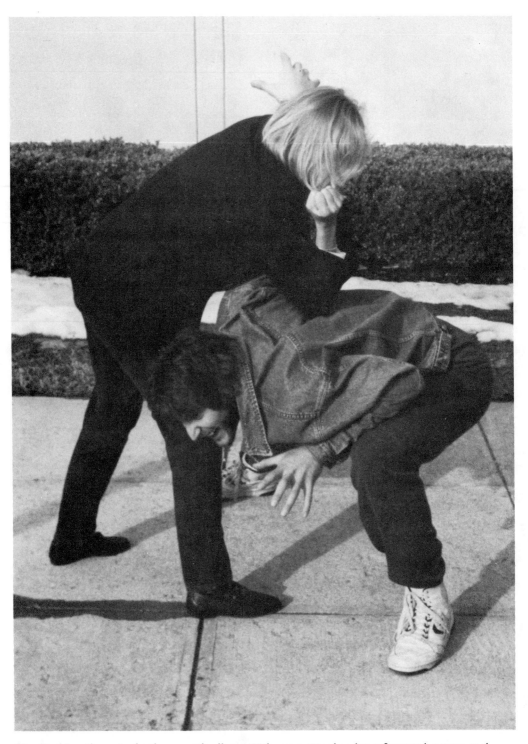

1 *Striking the spinal column with elbow. With your attacker bent forward, squat and drive your elbow straight down onto his spinal column.*

Striking the rib cage with (1) elbow, (2) fist, or (3) foot. With your feet shoulder-width apart, try to put your attacker in an outstretched position by pulling on his wrist as you make the strike.

❶

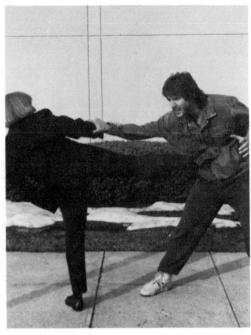

❷

❸

Striking the solar plexus with (1) elbow, (2) foot, or (3) knee. With the elbow and foot strikes, pull your attacker off balance and move forward with your strike. With the knee strike, pull his upper body down as you meet his midsection with your knee.

❶
Striking the kidney with (1) elbow or (2) punch. You should be slightly to the rear of your attacker, with your feet shoulder-width apart. Move toward your attacker as you strike.

❷

❶

Striking the spleen with (1) foot or (2) fist. When striking with the foot, always be sure to keep your balance and move toward your attacker. With the fist strike, keep one foot ahead of the other to get maximum power.

❷

Striking the bladder with (1) reverse hammer-fist or (2) elbow. With the hammer-fist strike, you must be low with your feet wide apart; strike in an upward motion. When you strike with the elbow to this area, drop to one knee and strike directly up. With both strikes, remember to keep your attacker outstretched by pulling out on his wrist.

Striking the diaphragm with (1) elbow or (2) hammer-fist. Keep one leg forward and the other back for strength and balance. Attempt to grab the back of your attacker's head and bring him forward into the strike.

①   **②**

Striking the collarbone with (1) elbow or (2) hammer-fist. Keep your feet apart in the horse rider's stance and strike straight down on top of your attacker's collarbone.

①   **②**

Striking and breaking the elbow with (1) forearm and outside wrist-lock or (2) armbar lock. With your attacker's wrist in an outside lock, pivot to that side so that one leg is in front of the other and drive your forearm directly into your attacker's elbow. To use an armbar lock, catch your attacker's arm over your shoulder so that his elbow is locked and pull toward yourself with both hands.

Striking the groin with (1) palm-hand, (2) ball or instep of foot, or (3) knee. Step forward and drive your palm up into your attacker's groin. To use your foot, grab your attacker and pull him toward you as you drive your foot into his groin. Use the knee when you are close to your attacker, for example, in a bear hug; just drive your knee up.

Striking the shin with (1) side kick or (2) heel of shoe. Hold on to your attacker so he cannot back away from the blow and simply drive either strike back into the shin.

Striking the back of the knee with (1) blade of foot or (2) heel kick. You should be behind your attacker, pulling him toward you by the hair or the collar. Aim both strikes directly into the back of his knee.

Striking the front of the knee with (1) side kick or (2) heel kick. Hold on to your attacker and pull him toward you as you drive your foot at his knee.

1 *Strike with the umbrella tip to the side of your attacker's throat under the jaw to the carotid artery. For maximum effect in this movement, your feet should be separated and you should strike with a forward thrust.*

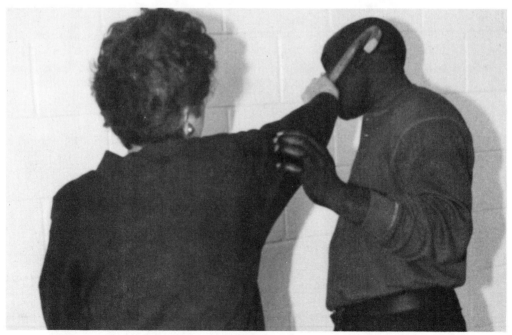

2 *Strike to your attacker's temple with the side of the cane.*

3 *Strike to your attacker's rib cage in a forward-lunging umbrella-tip strike. This strike is very effective when you are being grabbed in a two-handed choke from the front.*

4 *Using the cane, swing it directly up at your attacker's groin.*

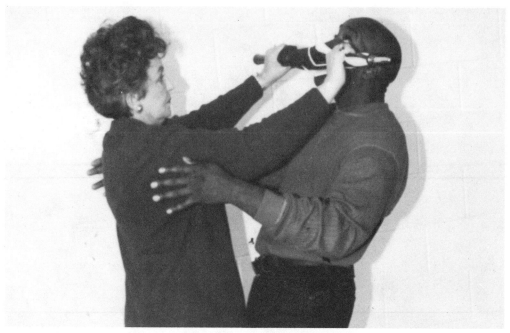

5 Strike to the bottom of your attacker's nose, driving your umbrella backward with both hands.

6 A forward-moving strike to your attacker's diaphragm (below the lower ribs) with the end of a cane.

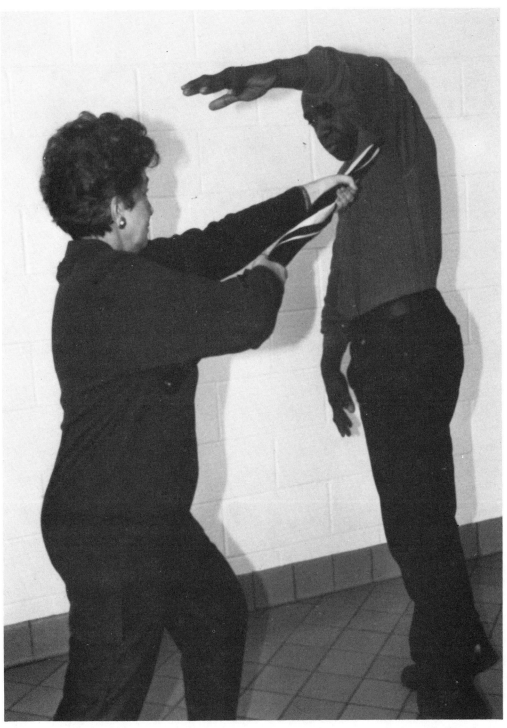

7 Strike to your attacker's armpit. Strike in an upward motion with the end of your umbrella, as if to lift your attacker directly up onto his toes.

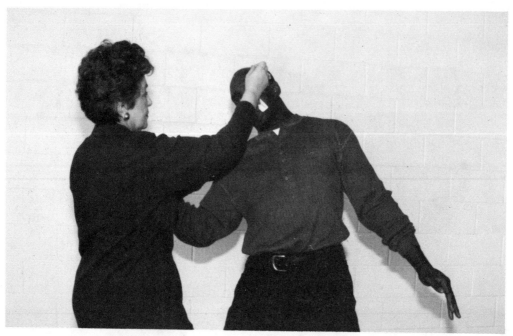

8 Your attacker is grabbing you, with your keys, strike directly to your attacker's eye sockets.

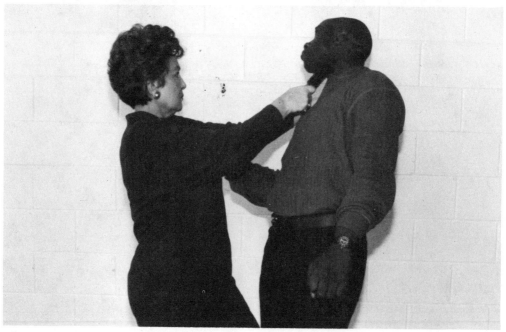

9 With a hairbrush, strike directly to your attacker's Adam's apple, holding either end of the hairbrush.

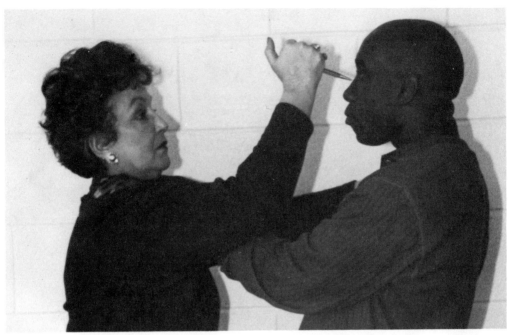

10 *Using a pen or pencil, you again aim for the eyes, but this time, drive your weapon directly into the eye.*

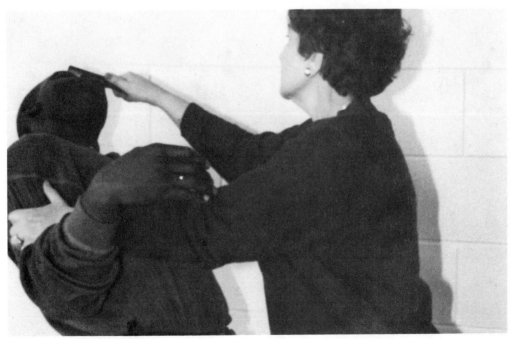

11 *With a comb, preferably a metal one, strike directly upward from your attacker's chin to his forehead or nose.*

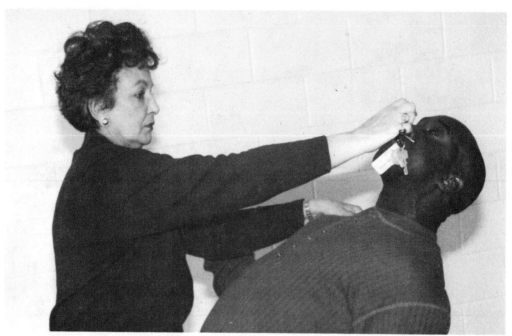

12 With your keys, strike directly upward under your attacker's nose or strike directly onto the bridge of his nose.

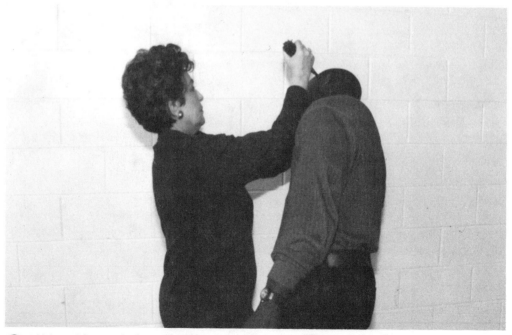

13 Using either end of your hairbrush, strike to your attacker's temple.

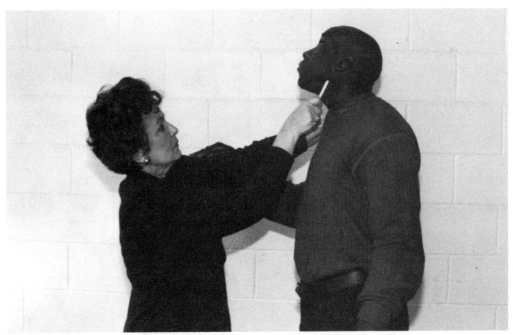

14 As you hold one side of your attacker's head with your hand, take your pen and drive it directly into the side of his neck (carotid artery).

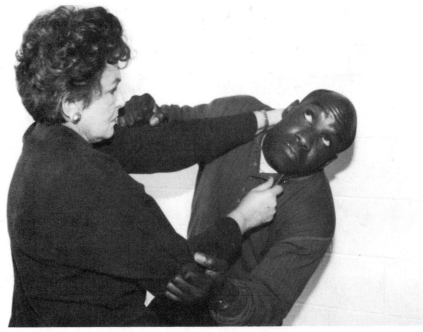

15 Taking your comb, strike directly under you attacker's neck in an upward motion. With this movement, you should be able to drive him backward.

ATTACK 1

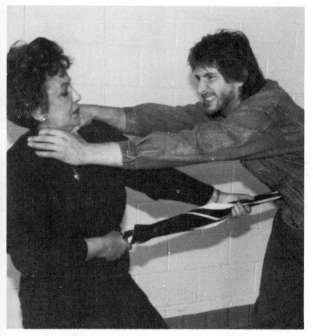

1

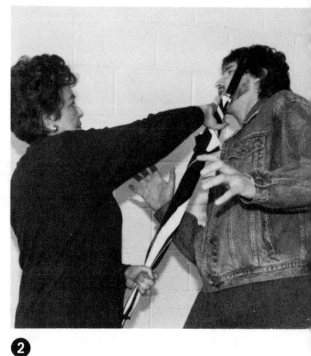

2

3

1—Your attacker has his hands gripped firmly around your neck and is choking you. Quickly drive the umbrella tip directly into your attacker's diaphragm.

2—Snap the other end of the umbrella around and straight into your attacker's face.

3—To complete the movement, continue your umbrella stride to the face in a downward motion.

ATTACK 2

1 Your attacker has grabbed you by the lapel with his right hand and is proceeding to draw you to him.

2 As your cane is in your right hand, you simply bring it across and in front of you, grabbing it with your left hand, palm down.

3 With the cane gripped firmly with both hands, strike straight down on top of your attacker's wrist or knuckles.

4 To complete the movement, take the cane and drive it directly upward to his throat. This should easily complete your defense.

ATTACK 3

1 As you are walking, an attacker on your left is placing his right arm around your shoulder and slowly forcing you to walk where he wants. With your umbrella in your right hand, simply pivot with both feet toward your attacker.

2 While turning, bring your umbrella up into your other hand and drive it into his midsection.

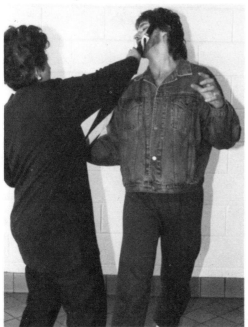

3 As your attacker is bent over in pain, take your right hand with the end of your umbrella and strike up into his face.

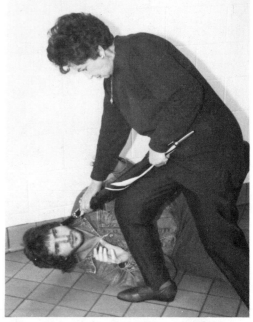

4 While striking to the facial area, step with your right foot behind your attacker and drive him straight down to the ground.

ATTACK 4

1 Your attacker has you firmly around the waist in a bear hug; as he applies pressure, you must act quickly by stamping with your heel to the instep of his foot.

2 Snap your right hand with your cane in an upward motion to the back of his head.

3 Strike your attacker to the back of his head, then grab the cane with your other hand and bring it down on the back of your attacker's neck. Keep constant pressure directly on his neck, which should be on your shoulder.

4 Drop to your right knee and pull your attacker down with direct pressure to the back of the neck.

ATTACK 5

 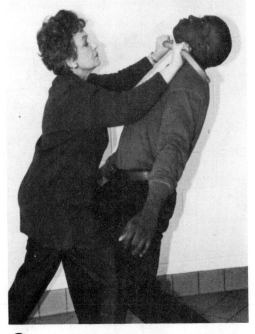

1—Your attacker is holding you firmly around the waist and your cane is in your right hand. Quickly snap the cane across to your left hand.

2—Strike with a rolling motion to your attacker's lower back. Your attacker is in pain and should release you.

3—Immediately bring your cane up and around to the front of his throat. You then complete the movement by hooking your attacker's left leg with your right leg, throwing him directly down with the cane pushing on his throat.

Conclusion

For a group of people brought up on the sound principles and strict observances as to ways of conducting oneself—including such dictums as:

1. **Stand proud**
2. **Be seen but not heard**
3. **Observe everything say nothing**

The need for self defense seminars come as a shock. Some probably will never be able to accept this - nobody can force another person to read, study, or practice skills involving active participation in crime prevention activities.

As a teacher, and advocate in anti-crime, self defense seminars for many years I recognize the growing need for everyone to become involved in just such a program.

Preventive programs in this area has become a dire necessity in the workplace, home, and recreation areas. Incidents leading to physical as well as emotional calamaties can be forestalled—if the warning signals are recognized in time.

"FIGHTING BACK" need not be a physical encounter. If it does come to that, knowing *where*, *what*, and *how* to strike is essential. The intention of this book is to point out various paths on different procedures making the actions of self protections a comfortable one for all.

ABOUT THE AUTHOR AND THE FUMA FEDERATION

A word about the Founder and Executive Director of FUMA; Michael DePasquale, Jr.:

The son of Michael Depasquale, Sr., Grandmaster (Shihan Soke) of the Yoshitsune Waza style of Ju-Jitsu, and one of the founders of Ju-Jitsu in the US, Michael DePasquale, Jr.'s Martial Arts career began in early childhood with Yoshitsune Waza in which he presently holds the coveted rank of Master of the Second Rank (Ni Dai Shihan). During over 30 years of study, practice, competition and teaching in the Martial Arts he has also attained 5th degree Black Belt level in Hakko-Ryu Ju-Jitsu and holds advanced Black Belts in Karate and Judo. A tireless competitor during the 70's and 80's, Michael was honored by Official Karate Magazine as Martial Arts Star of the Year in 1977/78, he won the AAU East Karate Championship in 1981, and qualified for the Pan American Team Trials. His prolonged interest in self-defense has also led Michael to develop his own self-defense style, DePasquale Combat Ju-Jitsu, which has been accepted as a Martial Art in its own right.

In addition, Michael is the Publisher/Editor of Karate International Magazine which he created in 1989 and has appeared on numerous television and radio shows, such as Regis Philbin, Yo MTV Raps, Nickelodeon, Attitudes and the Network News speaking about F.U.M.A.'s Streetwise Safety and Self Defense techniques and seminars.

Michael has also taught the 1st Division Of The Army Special Forces, FBI, U.S. Marshals, Postal Police and many other law enforcement personnel. He has appeared in such movies as "KING OF THE KICK BOXERS," "AMERICAN SHOALIN" AND STARRED IN "CHINA HEAT" PAID IN BLOOD. To date Michael has also been inducted in 6 different Martial Art Halls of Fame. Besides publishing six books with Simon & Shuster, Michael continues to be in demand internationally for his anti-crime self-defense seminars.

You can reach Michael Depasquale Jr. at (201) 573-8028.

THE FEDERATION OF UNITED MARTIAL ARTISTS (FUMA)

Americans have every reason to believe that crime is the leading problem in America today!

According to the FBI's Uniform Crime Report (1), a crime is committed every 2 seconds; every 17 seconds a violent crime is committed, with an aggravated assault every 29 seconds, and a robbery every 46 seconds. Once every 5 minutes a rape occurs and violent crime is increasing rapidly!

The Federation of United Martial Artists (FUMA), a charitable not-for-profit organization registered with the US Internal Revenue Service (2), was founded in 1984 by Michael DePasquale, Jr., internationally known Martial Artist, film star and publisher, to unite Martial Artists in providing law abiding citizens with proactive programs of education and training in crime awareness and self-defense.

As a result of the effort of Michael DePasquale, Jr., since 1984, FUMA membership has grown to include over 1500 leading masters, instructors, students, representing all the Martial Arts as well as concerned citizens who are actively working to make the streets of America safer. FUMA members are engaged in conducting crime awareness and self-defense seminars and training courses, and participating in a variety of other civic activities, throughout the United States and in many foreign countries.

THE FUMA MISSION:

FUMA seeks to focus the enormous positive potential of the Martial Arts world on a single common goal which must certainly be acceptable to everyone: public safety through education.

FUMA fights crime through a proactive approach to personal safety. This approach—aimed at people from all walks of life—features educational opportunities designed to:

- promote awareness.
- develop knowledge and skills for conflict avoidance and resolution and personal protection.
- foster positive personal and civic values and behavior among youth.

WHO ARE FUMA'S CLIENTS?

FUMA has served a wide variety of community service and charitable groups; the handicapped and senior citizens, students in grade school, high school and college, health and law enforcement professionals and military personnel.

HOW DOES FUMA SERVE?

FUMA serves the community through a diversity of activities, examples of which follow:

EDUCATION AND TRAINING

Seminars and Courses:

Seminars on personal protection, home security and corporate crime prevention.

Special proactive personal safety training, tailored to the special needs of groups such as children, senior citizens and the handicapped.

Training in street survival tactics for law enforcement personnel.

Public Information:

Production and distribution of materials on personal safety measures.

Cooperation with local press, government, education and law enforcement in raising awareness.

Self-defense and crime awareness programs on major television programs and networks.
Personal TV and radio appearances by FUMA members.
Newspaper reports on FUMA activities.

COMMUNITY SERVICE

FUMA supports public information programs related to the FUMA mission conducted by government, civic, church or synagogue, law enforcement or commercial groups seeking assistance, e.g., Volunteer Centers, Councils on Aging, the Salvation Army, Rape Crisis Centers, Women's Clubs, and Anti-Drug Campaigns.

FUNDING AND FUTURE PLANS

FUMA's long-range goal is to provide no-cost services to governmental entities, not-for-profit foundations and civic organizations, and to provide minimum-cost assistance to commercial organizations participating in anti-crime activities.

To achieve these goals, we need additional funding to:

• Expand the FUMA funding base to support long-distance travel fees for members to assist civic or charitable organizations which request our support.

• Upgrade FUMA office equipment.

• Support a small part-time staff to better coordinate FUMA activities.

• Support development of additional training and educational materials.

We earnestly solicit financial or material support from corporations, foundations, and all concerned individuals. Material support may include office equipment and supplies or anti-crime educational materials. Please note: All contributions to FUMA are tax-deductible, under Section 170 of the IRS code.

FOR FURTHER INFORMATION ABOUT FUMA MEMBERSHIP, FUMA SERVICES, CONTRIBUTIONS TO FUMA OR TO ARRANGE A STREET-WISE SAFETY AND SELF-DEFENSE SEMINAR FOR YOUR CLUB OR ORGANIZATION PLEASE CONTACT:

MICHAEL DEPASQUALE, JR.
EXECUTIVE DIRECTOR
FEDERATION OF UNITED MARTIAL ARTISTS
P.O. BOX 8585—WOODCLIFF LAKE, NEW JERSEY 07675
201-573-8028
OR
DR. ROBERT C. SUGGS
2507 CULPEPER ROAD—ALEXANDRIA, VIRGINIA 22308